The TIMELESS ROSARY

The
TIMELESS
ROSARY

BRIAN JOSEPH HORAN

Leonine Publishers
Phoenix, Arizona

The Scripture citations used in this work are taken from the *New American Bible* (Washington, D.C.: World Catholic Press, 1986; part of WORDsearch CROSS e-book).

Published by Leonine Publishers LLC
PO Box 8099
Phoenix, Arizona 85066

ISBN-13: 978-0-9859483-7-5

10 9 8 7 6 5 4 3 2

Printed in the United States of America

Library of Congress Control Number: 2012949230

Visit us online at www.leoninepublishers.com
For more information: info@leoninepublishers.com

ACKNOWLEDGEMENTS

Patricia Anne Baylog—who inspired me to write my thoughts on the timelessness of the Rosary mysteries and to share them with our shepherd, Bishop David O'Connell.

Bishop David O'Connell—for taking the time to review my book, writing the foreword, and sending it out with his blessing.

Father Michael Burns, Father John Campoli, Father Jeff Kegley, and all the priests, sisters, and deacons—for reviewing the book and providing me with guidance and encouragement.

All the members of Saint Mary's prayer group—who helped with editing and proofing my manuscript.

Angela Barbalace—for the beautiful original artwork found throughout the book, depicting the timeless nature of the mysteries.

Leonine Publishers—for agreeing to take on the manuscript, turning my ideas into professional design work, and turning it into the book now in your hands.

Earl and Paul Alger—for a wonderful job in making CDs for the seven different Rosary blends, as well as the beautiful website at www.timelessrosary.com where the audio files can be obtained.

Countless others—who helped me with this labor of love.

I am eternally grateful, and may God bless each of you who helped with this endeavor.

CONTENTS

May God bless all, who use *The Timeless Rosary* for prayer,
with many blessings.

~ Most Reverend David M. O'Connell, C.M.

FOREWORD

The *Catechism of the Catholic Church* reminds us that, "the Church's devotion to the Blessed Virgin is intrinsic to Christian worship. ... From the most ancient times the Blessed Virgin Mary has been honored with the title of 'Mother of God,' to whose protection the faithful fly in all their dangers and needs. ... Marian prayer, such as the rosary, an 'epitome of the whole gospel,' expresses this devotion to the Virgin Mary" (*CCC*, no. 971).

This beautiful paragraph from our *Catechism* came to mind as I read *Timeless Rosary*. The organization of prayers and the citation of scriptural references richly complement this traditional devotion Catholics knew, loved, and prayed "from the most ancient times."

As with many things in the Church's long history, the origin of the rosary is sometimes disputed. Tradition attributes its beginnings to an apparition of the Blessed Virgin Mary to Saint Dominic, who lived from AD 1170–1221. Saint Dominic founded the Order of Preachers, popularly known by the name "Dominicans." At the very least, we know that this devotion gradually developed and fostered by members of his Order. The structure of the prayer we know today, with fifteen decades—three sets of five each, named for the Joyful, Sorrowful, and Glorious mysteries of Christ's life—became normative throughout the Catholic world by the 16th century papacy of Pope Pius V. The rosary continued unchanged for the next four centuries, with occasional prayers and meditations added or subtracted by local custom. In 2002, however, Blessed Pope John Paul II presented a fourth set of mysteries, the Luminous Mysteries, for the devotion of the faithful.

Devotion to the Blessed Virgin Mary through her rosary has served to lead many believers—and even some non-believers, thanks to this powerful prayer—to the heart of her Son, Jesus Christ. Devotion to Mary, yes, the way any son or daughter is "devoted" to his or her mother. But worship and the path offered by this *timeless* prayer are focused on the Lord Jesus Christ, the One Who first called her "Mother" and through whose intercession we pray the rosary.

The Timeless Rosary enriches what already is and has always been a rich source of grace and blessing in the Church through Marian prayer and devotion. May those who use this new prayer aid find the path to Jesus Christ through the intercession of our Blessed Mother Mary.

~Most Reverend David M. O'Connell, C.M.
Bishop of Trenton, July, 2011

INTRODUCTION

Dedicated to Our Blessed Mother

God is a timeless Spirit, Who resides in His eternal now, without beginning, without end. It is only because of His great Love for us that He subjects Himself to the sequential bonds of time as the Word Incarnate. Born of the Virgin Mary, Jesus comes into time to save and to reconcile the Father's creation from the bondage of sin and eternal damnation. God the Father, in doing this, teaches, governs, and sanctifies us by the life, death, and resurrection of His Son, Jesus, and the Holy Catholic Church He founded.

The traditional Rosary is a presentation of the mysteries of our redemption, given sequentially, and expanded by Blessed Pope John Paul II, to illuminate the perfect knowledge of God, Who is Love. What would happen if we enter into the Sacred Mysteries of the Rosary of our Redemption in a timeless way? Would there be a universal, mystical connection if all the first, second, third, fourth, and fifth mysteries are juxtaposed to enable a more timeless, rather than sequential consideration?

Would this method of focus allow us to better grasp the complete mystery, or at least a fuller picture of God's timeless Love for us?

I invite you as well: Enter in.

Rosary Prayers

Prayers said at the beginning and at the end of each rosary

1. Lovely Lady Dressed in Blue

Lovely Lady dressed in blue,
Teach me how to pray!
God was just your little Boy,
Tell me what to say!
Did you lift Him up, sometimes,
Gently, on your knee?
Did you sing to Him the way,
Mother does to me?
Did you hold His hand at night?
Did you ever try
Telling stories of the world?
O! And did He cry?
Do you really think He cares
If I tell Him things,
Little things that happen? And
Do the Angels' wings
Make a noise? And can He hear
Me if I speak low?
Does He understand me now?
Tell me—for you know.
Lovely Lady dressed in blue,
Teach me how to pray!
God was just your little Boy
And you know the way.

(Mary Dixon Thayer)

2. Come, Holy Spirit

Come, Holy Spirit, Creator blest,
And in our souls take up Thy rest;
Come with Thy grace and heavenly aid
To fill the hearts which Thou hast made.

O comforter, to Thee we cry,
O heavenly gift of God Most High,
O fount of life and fire of love,
And sweet anointing from above.

Thou in Thy sevenfold gifts are known;
The finger of God's hand we own;
The promise of the Father, Thou
Who dost the tongue with power endow.

Kindle our senses from above,
And make our hearts overflow with love;
With patience firm and virtue high
The weaknesses of our flesh supply.

Far from us drive the foe we dread,
And grant us Thy peace instead;
So shall we not, with Thee for guide,
Turn from the path of life aside.

Oh, may Thy grace on us bestow
The Father and the Son to know;
And Thee, through endless times confessed,
Of both the eternal Spirit blest.

All glory while the ages run,
Be to the Father and the Son,
Who rose from death; the same to Thee
Oh Holy Spirit, eternally.
Amen.

3. Hail Star of the Sea

Hail bright star of ocean,
God's own Mother blest,
Ever sinless Virgin,
Gate of heavenly rest.

Taking that sweet Ave
Which from Gabriel came,
Peace confirm within us,
Changing Eva's name.

Break the captives' fetters,
Light on blindness pour,
All our ills expelling,
Every bliss implore.

Show thyself a Mother;
May the Word Divine,
Born for us thy Infant,
Hear our prayers through thine.

Virgin all excelling,
Mildest of the mild,
Freed from guilt, preserve us,
Pure and undefiled.

Keep our life all spotless,
Make our way secure,
Till we find in Jesus
Joy forevermore.

Through the highest heaven
To the Almighty Three,
Father, Son, and Spirit
One same glory be, Amen.

4. Let Us Pray

O God, whose only begotten Son, by His life, death, and resurrection, has purchased for us the rewards of eternal life, grant, we beseech Thee, that while meditating upon these mysteries of the Most Holy Rosary of the Blessed Virgin Mary, we may both imitate what they contain and obtain what they promise, through the same Christ our Lord. Amen.

The Sign of the Cross
In the name of the Father and of the Son and of the Holy Ghost. Amen.

Apostles' Creed
I believe in God, the Father Almighty, Creator of Heaven and earth; and in Jesus Christ, His only Son, our Lord; (Bow) Who was conceived by the Holy Spirit, born of the Virgin Mary, suffered under Pontius Pilate, was crucified, died and was buried. He descended into hell. On the third day He arose again from the dead. He ascended into Heaven, and is seated at the right hand of God, the Father Almighty; from there He will come to judge the living and the dead. I believe in the Holy Spirit, the Holy Catholic Church, the communion of saints, the forgiveness of sins, the resurrection of the body, and life everlasting. Amen.

Our Father
Our Father, Who art in Heaven, hallowed be Thy name, Thy kingdom come; Thy will be done on earth as it is in Heaven. Give us this day our daily bread; and forgive us our trespasses as we forgive those who trespass against us; and lead us not into temptation, but deliver us from evil. Amen.

Hail Mary
Hail Mary, full of grace! The Lord is with Thee; blessed art thou among women, and blessed is the fruit of thy womb, Jesus. Holy Mary, Mother of God, pray for us sinners, now and at the hour of our death. Amen.

Glory Be

Glory be to the Father, and to the Son, and to the Holy Spirit. As it was in the beginning, is now and ever shall be, world without end. Amen.

Fatima Prayer

O my Jesus, forgive us our sins, save us from the fires of hell, and lead all souls to Heaven, especially those in most need of Your Mercy.

Hail, Holy Queen

Hail, holy Queen, Mother of Mercy! Our life, our sweetness, and our hope! To thee do we cry, poor banished children of Eve; to thee do we send up our sighs, mourning and weeping in this valley, of tears. Turn, then, most gracious advocate, thine eyes of mercy toward us; and after this our exile show unto us the blessed fruit of thy womb, Jesus; O clement, O loving, O sweet Virgin Mary.

Pray for us, O holy Mother of God, that we may be made worthy of the promises of Christ.

Saint Michael Prayer

Saint Michael the Archangel, defend us in battle. Be our protection against the wickedness and snares of the devil. May God rebuke him, we humbly pray; and do thou, O Prince of the Heavenly Host, by the power of God, cast into hell Satan, and all the evil spirits, who prowl around the world seeking the ruin of souls. Amen.

FAITH
Hebrews 11:1-3, 6

[1] Faith is the realization of what is hoped for and evidence of things not seen. [2] Because of it the ancients were well attested. [3] By faith we understand that the universe was ordered by the word of God, so that what is visible came into being through the invisible.

[6] But without faith it is impossible to please him, for anyone who approaches God must believe that he exists and that he rewards those who seek him.

HOPE
Romans 8:14-28

[14] For those who are led by the Spirit of God are children of God. [15] For you did not receive a spirit of slavery to fall back into fear, but you received a spirit of adoption, through which we cry, "Abba, Father!" [16] The Spirit itself bears witness with our spirit that we are children of God, [17] and if children, then heirs, heirs of God and joint heirs with Christ, if only we suffer with him so that we may also be glorified with him. [18] I consider that the sufferings of this present time are as nothing compared with the glory to be revealed for us. [19] For creation awaits with eager expectation the revelation of the children of God; [20] for creation was made subject to futility, not of its own accord but because of the one who subjected it, in hope [21] that creation itself would be set free from slavery to corruption and share in the glorious freedom of the children of God. [22] We know that all creation is groaning in labor pains even until now; [23] and not only that, but we ourselves, who have the firstfruits of the Spirit, we also groan within ourselves as we wait for adoption, the redemption of our bodies. [24] For in hope we were saved. Now hope that sees for itself is not hope. For who hopes for what one sees? [25] But if we hope for what we do not see, we wait with endurance.

[26] In the same way, the Spirit too comes to the aid of our weakness; for we do not know how to pray as we ought, but the Spirit itself intercedes with inexpressible groaning. [27] And the one who searches hearts knows what is the intention of the Spirit, because it intercedes for the holy ones according to God's will.

²⁸ We know that all things work for good for those who love God, who are called according to his purpose.

LOVE
1 Corinthians 13:1-13

¹ If I speak in human and angelic tongues but do not have love, I am a resounding gong or a clashing cymbal. ² And if I have the gift of prophecy and comprehend all mysteries and all knowledge; if I have all faith so as to move mountains but do not have love, I am nothing. ³ If I give away everything I own, and if I hand my body over so that I may boast but do not have love, I gain nothing.

⁴ Love is patient, love is kind. It is not jealous, [love] is not pompous, it is not inflated, ⁵ it is not rude, it does not seek its own interests, it is not quick-tempered, it does not brood over injury, ⁶ it does not rejoice over wrongdoing but rejoices with the truth. ⁷ It bears all things, believes all things, hopes all things, and endures all things.

⁸ Love never fails. If there are prophecies, they will be brought to nothing; if tongues, they will cease; if knowledge, it will be brought to nothing. ⁹ For we know partially and we prophesy partially, ¹⁰ but when the perfect comes, the partial will pass away. ¹¹ When I was a child, I used to talk as a child, think as a child, reason as a child; when I became a man, I put aside childish things. ¹² At present we see indistinctly, as in a mirror, but then face to face. At present I know partially; then I shall know fully, as I am fully known. ¹³ So faith, hope, love remain, these three; but the greatest of these is love.

Praise and Worship

THE TIMELESS PRAISE AND WORSHIP ROSARY

The Timeless Praise and Worship Rosary blends the traditional prayers of the Rosary, viewed in a timeless way, with an expression of praise and worship to the Lord. It can be a very powerful and enlightening way of expressing our appreciation to God. We do this by praising and worshiping Him while meditating on the mysteries of His love and our redemption.

This is your chance to be as the one, grateful leper, who went back to thank the Lord for healing him.

This can also be a good Rosary to add intercessory prayers for others, as it inspires love of neighbor. We can show our own appreciation to God for all He did for us, by imitating Him and helping others with our prayers.

This Rosary may be prayed while visiting our Eucharistic Lord at an adoration chapel, on the way to and from work, on a plane, at the park, during a visit to a prison, at a hospital, on a bus, in church, at home, in bed, or anytime you are feeling grateful or blessed.

Rosary Reflections

1. **Lovely Lady dressed in blue...** (pg. 1)
2. **Come, Holy Spirit...** (pg. 2)
3. **Hail bright star of ocean...** (pg. 3)
4. **Let us pray. Oh God, whose only begotten Son...** (pg. 4)
5. (Sign of the Cross)
   In the Name of the Father...

I Believe in God... (Apostles' Creed, pg. 4)

Our Father...

Hail Mary...
Jesus, we ask You for an increase in the gift of Faith:
(Hebrews 11:1-3, 6, pg. 6)
Holy Mary...

Hail Mary...
Jesus, we ask You for an increase in the gift of Hope:
(Romans 8:14-28, pg. 6)
Holy Mary...

Hail Mary...
Jesus, we ask You for an increase in the gift of Love:
(1 Corinthians 13:1-13, pg. 7)
Holy Mary...

Glory be...

Oh my Jesus... (Fatima Prayer, pg. 5)

The First Sacred Mysteries of the Rosary of our Redemption

The joy of the Annunciation was illuminated by Your Baptism. You ransomed us through the sorrow and shedding of Your blood during the Agony in the Garden and revealed our redemption in Your Glorious Resurrection.

Our Father...

1. Hail Mary...

Jesus, we thank You Lord, and we ask You to send us Your Holy Spirit to enlighten us in our understanding of these mysteries of our redemption;

Holy Mary...

2. Hail Mary...

Jesus in the mystery of the Annunciation, we thank You Lord;

Holy Mary...

3. Hail Mary...

Jesus in the mystery of the Annunciation, we thank You Lord;

Holy Mary...

4. Hail Mary...

Jesus in the mystery of Your Baptism, we thank You Lord;

Holy Mary...

5. Hail Mary...

Jesus in the mystery of Your Baptism, we thank You Lord;

Holy Mary...

6. Hail Mary...

Jesus in the mystery of the Agony in the Garden, we thank You Lord;

Holy Mary...

7. Hail Mary...

Jesus in the mystery of the Agony in the Garden, we thank You Lord;

Holy Mary...

8. Hail Mary...

Jesus in the mystery of Your Resurrection, we thank You Lord;

Holy Mary...

9. Hail Mary...

Jesus in the mystery of Your Resurrection, we thank You Lord;

Holy Mary...

10. Hail Mary...

Jesus, we thank You Lord, and we ask You for an increase in the gifts of the Holy Spirit: that we may come to know You clearer, follow You nearer, and love You dearer;

Holy Mary...

Glory be...

Oh my Jesus...

The Second Sacred Mysteries of the Rosary of our Redemption

The joy of the Visitation was illuminated by Your miracle at the Wedding Feast of Cana. You ransomed us through the sorrow and shedding of Your blood during the Scourging at the Pillar and revealed our redemption in Your Glorious Ascension.

Our Father...

1. Hail Mary...
Jesus, we praise You Lord, and we ask You to send us Your Holy Spirit to enlighten us in our understanding of these mysteries of our redemption;
Holy Mary...

2. Hail Mary...
Jesus in the mystery of the Visitation, we praise You Lord;
Holy Mary...

3. Hail Mary...
Jesus in the mystery of the Visitation, we praise You Lord;
Holy Mary...

4. Hail Mary...
Jesus in the mystery of the Wedding Feast at Cana, we praise You Lord;
Holy Mary...

5. Hail Mary...
Jesus in the mystery of the Wedding Feast at Cana, we praise You Lord;
Holy Mary...

6. Hail Mary...
Jesus in the mystery of the Scourging at the Pillar, we praise You Lord;
Holy Mary...

7. Hail Mary...
Jesus in the mystery of the Scourging at the Pillar, we praise You Lord;
Holy Mary...

8. Hail Mary...
Jesus in the mystery of Your Ascension, we praise You Lord;
Holy Mary...

9. Hail Mary...
Jesus in the mystery of Your Ascension, we praise You Lord;
Holy Mary...

10. Hail Mary...
Jesus, we praise You Lord, and we ask You for an increase in the gifts of the Holy Spirit: that we may come to know You clearer, follow You nearer, and love You dearer;
Holy Mary...

Glory be...

Oh my Jesus...

THE THIRD
SACRED MYSTERIES
OF THE ROSARY OF OUR
REDEMPTION

The joy of the Nativity was illuminated by Your proclamation of the Gospels. You ransomed us through the sorrow and shedding of Your blood during the Crowning with Thorns and revealed our redemption in the Glorious Descent of the Holy Spirit.

Our Father...

1. Hail Mary...
Jesus, we adore You Lord, and we ask You to send us Your Holy Spirit to enlighten us in our understanding of these mysteries of our redemption;
Holy Mary...

2. Hail Mary...
Jesus in the mystery of the Nativity, we adore You Lord;
Holy Mary...

3. Hail Mary...
Jesus in the mystery of the Nativity, we adore You Lord;
Holy Mary...

4. Hail Mary...
Jesus in the mystery of Your proclamation of the Gospels, we adore You Lord;
Holy Mary...

5. Hail Mary...
Jesus in the mystery of Your proclamation of the Gospels, we adore You Lord;
Holy Mary...

6. Hail Mary...
   Jesus in the mystery of the Crowning with Thorns, we adore You Lord;
   Holy Mary...

7. Hail Mary...
   Jesus in the mystery of the Crowning with Thorns, we adore You Lord;
   Holy Mary...

8. Hail Mary...
   Jesus in the mystery of the Descent of the Holy Spirit, we adore You Lord;
   Holy Mary...

9. Hail Mary...
   Jesus in the mystery of the Descent of the Holy Spirit, we adore You Lord;
   Holy Mary...

10. Hail Mary...
   Jesus, we adore You Lord, and we ask You for an increase in the gifts of the Holy Spirit: that we may come to know You clearer, follow You nearer, and love You dearer;
   Holy Mary...

Glory be...

Oh my Jesus...

THE FOURTH
SACRED MYSTERIES
OF THE ROSARY OF OUR
REDEMPTION

The joy of the Presentation was illuminated by Your Transfiguration. You ransomed us through the sorrow and shedding of Your blood during the Carrying of the Cross and revealed our redemption in the Glorious Assumption of Your Blessed Mother into heaven.

Our Father...

1. Hail Mary...
Jesus, we worship You Lord, and we ask You to send us Your Holy Spirit to enlighten us in our understanding of these mysteries of our redemption;
Holy Mary...

2. Hail Mary...
Jesus in the mystery of the Presentation, we worship You Lord;
Holy Mary...

3. Hail Mary...
Jesus in the mystery of the Presentation, we worship You Lord;
Holy Mary...

4. Hail Mary...
Jesus in the mystery of Your Transfiguration, we worship You Lord;
Holy Mary...

5. Hail Mary...
Jesus in the mystery of Your Transfiguration, we worship You Lord;
Holy Mary...

6. Hail Mary...
   Jesus in the mystery of the Carrying of the Cross, we worship You Lord;
   Holy Mary...

7. Hail Mary...
   Jesus in the mystery of the Carrying of the Cross, we worship You Lord;
   Holy Mary...

8. Hail Mary...
   Jesus in the mystery of the Assumption of Your Blessed Mother into heaven, we worship You Lord;
   Holy Mary...

9. Hail Mary...
   Jesus in the mystery of the Assumption of Your Blessed Mother into heaven, we worship You Lord;
   Holy Mary...

10. Hail Mary...
   Jesus, we worship You Lord, and we ask You for an increase in the gifts of the Holy Spirit: that we may come to know You clearer, follow You nearer, and love You dearer;
   Holy Mary...

Glory be...

Oh my Jesus...

The Fifth
Sacred Mysteries
of the Rosary of our
Redemption

The joy of Finding the Child Jesus in the Temple was illuminated by Your Institution of the Eucharist. You ransomed us through the sorrow and shedding of Your blood in the Crucifixion and revealed our redemption in the Glorious Coronation of Your Blessed Mother as Queen of Heaven and Earth.

Our Father...

1. Hail Mary...
Jesus, we love You Lord, and we ask You to send us Your Holy Spirit to enlighten us in our understanding of these mysteries of our redemption;
Holy Mary...

2. Hail Mary...
Jesus in the mystery of Finding the Child Jesus in the Temple, we love You Lord;
Holy Mary...

3. Hail Mary...
Jesus in the mystery of Finding the Child Jesus in the Temple, we love You Lord;
Holy Mary...

4. Hail Mary...
Jesus in the mystery of Your Institution of the Eucharist, we love You Lord;
Holy Mary...

5. Hail Mary...
Jesus in the mystery of Your Institution of the Eucharist, we love You Lord;
Holy Mary...

6. Hail Mary...
Jesus in the mystery of the Crucifixion, we love You Lord;
Holy Mary...

7. Hail Mary...
Jesus in the mystery of the Crucifixion, we love You Lord;
Holy Mary...

8. Hail Mary...

Jesus in the mystery of the Coronation of Your Blessed Mother as Queen of Heaven and Earth, we love You Lord; **Holy Mary...**

9. Hail Mary...

Jesus in the mystery of the Coronation of Your Blessed Mother as Queen of Heaven and Earth, we love You Lord; **Holy Mary...**

10. Hail Mary...

Jesus, we love You Lord, and we ask You for an increase in the gifts of the Holy Spirit: that we may come to know You clearer, follow You nearer, and love You dearer; **Holy Mary...**

Glory be...

Oh my Jesus...

Hail, Holy Queen... (pg. 5)

Let us pray. Oh God, whose only begotten Son... (pg. 4)

St. Michael the Archangel... (pg. 5)

For the intentions of the Holy Father:

    Our Father...

    Hail Mary...

    Glory be...

In the beginning was the Word... (pg. 209)

THE TIMELESS SPIRITUAL FRUITS ROSARY

The Timeless Spiritual Fruits Rosary blends the traditional prayers of the Rosary, viewed in a timeless way, with a petition for the fruits of the Holy Spirit, which correspond to each mystery. It can be a very powerful and enlightening way of communicating with our God, by meditating on the mysteries of our redemption and petitioning Him for the fruits gained by them.

This Rosary can be prayed at anytime, but is especially good to pray when feeling down, depressed, lonely, unloved, and unlovable. In any case, you will always finish your Rosary filled with joy and a better knowledge of God's great Love for you. You see, by asking your Heavenly Father for these gifts, you bring Him joy, for He loves to give them to His children so they may better share in His joy.

Rosary Reflections

1. **Lovely Lady dressed in blue...** (pg. 1)

2. **Come, Holy Spirit...** (pg. 2)

3. **Hail bright star of ocean...** (pg. 3)

4. **Let us pray. Oh God, whose only begotten Son...** (pg. 4)

5. (Sign of the Cross) **In the name of the Father...**

I Believe in God... (Apostles' Creed, pg. 4)

Our Father...

Hail Mary...
Jesus, we ask You for an increase in the gift of Faith:
(Hebrews 11:1-3, 6, pg. 6)
Holy Mary...

Hail Mary...
Jesus, we ask You for an increase in the gift of Hope:
(Romans 8:14-28, pg. 6)
Holy Mary...

Hail Mary...
Jesus, we ask You for an increase in the gift of Love:
(1 Corinthians 13:1-13, pg. 7)
Holy Mary...

Glory be...

Oh my Jesus... (Fatima Prayer, pg. 5)

THE FIRST
SACRED MYSTERIES
OF THE ROSARY OF OUR
REDEMPTION

The joy of the Annunciation was illuminated by Your Baptism. You ransomed us through the sorrow and shedding of Your blood during the Agony in the Garden and revealed our redemption in Your Glorious Resurrection.

Our Father...

1. Hail Mary...
Jesus, we ask You to send us Your Holy Spirit to enlighten us in our understanding of these mysteries of our redemption;
Holy Mary...

2 Hail Mary...
Jesus in the mystery of the Annunciation, we pray for the spiritual fruit of humility;
Holy Mary...

3. Hail Mary...
Jesus in the mystery of the Annunciation, we pray for the spiritual fruit of discernment;
Holy Mary...

4. Hail Mary...
Jesus in the mystery of Your Baptism, we pray for the spiritual fruit of trust;
Holy Mary...

5. Hail Mary...
Jesus in the mystery of Your Baptism, we pray for the spiritual fruit of surrender;
Holy Mary...

6. Hail Mary...

>Jesus in the mystery of the Agony in the Garden, we pray for the spiritual fruit of patient submission to God's will;
>**Holy Mary...**

7. Hail Mary...

>Jesus in the mystery of the Agony in the Garden, we pray for the spiritual fruit of a daily holy hour;
>**Holy Mary...**

8. Hail Mary...

>Jesus in the mystery of Your Resurrection, we pray for the spiritual fruit of holiness;
>**Holy Mary...**

9. Hail Mary...

>Jesus in the mystery of Your Resurrection, we pray for the spiritual fruit of selflessness;
>**Holy Mary...**

10. Hail Mary...

>Jesus, we ask You for an increase in the gifts of the Holy Spirit: that we may come to know You clearer, follow You nearer, and love You dearer;
>**Holy Mary...**

Glory be...

Oh my Jesus...

THE SECOND SACRED MYSTERIES OF THE ROSARY OF OUR REDEMPTION

The joy of the Visitation was illuminated by Your miracle at the Wedding Feast of Cana. You ransomed us through the sorrow and shedding of Your blood during the Scourging at the Pillar and revealed our redemption in Your Glorious Ascension.

Our Father...

1. Hail Mary...
Jesus, we ask You to send us Your Holy Spirit to enlighten us in our understanding of these mysteries of our redemption;
Holy Mary...

2. Hail Mary...
Jesus in the mystery of the Visitation, we pray for the spiritual fruit of love of neighbor;
Holy Mary...

3. Hail Mary...
Jesus in the mystery of the Visitation, we pray for the spiritual fruit of love and compassion;
Holy Mary...

4. Hail Mary...
Jesus in the mystery of the Wedding Feast at Cana, we pray for the spiritual fruit of fidelity;
Holy Mary...

5. Hail Mary...
Jesus in the mystery of the Wedding Feast at Cana, we pray for the spiritual fruit of obedience to Jesus;
Holy Mary...

6. Hail Mary...

Jesus in the mystery of the Scourging at the Pillar, we pray for the spiritual fruit of mortification of the senses;
Holy Mary...

7. Hail Mary...

Jesus in the mystery of the Scourging at the Pillar, we pray for the spiritual fruits which come from allowing all human suffering throughout time to be offered up in union with the passion of Jesus Christ for the sake of His body, the Church;
Holy Mary...

8. Hail Mary...

Jesus in the mystery of Your Ascension, we pray for the spiritual fruit of growth and transformation;
Holy Mary...

9. Hail Mary...

Jesus in the mystery of Your Ascension, we pray for the spiritual fruit of ascending to the Father;
Holy Mary...

10. Hail Mary...

Jesus, we ask You for an increase in the gifts of the Holy Spirit: that we may come to know You clearer, follow You nearer, and love You dearer;
Holy Mary...

Glory be...

Oh my Jesus...

THE THIRD
SACRED MYSTERIES
OF THE ROSARY OF OUR
REDEMPTION

The joy of the Nativity was illuminated by Your proclamation of the Gospels. You ransomed us through the sorrow and shedding of Your blood during the Crowning with Thorns and revealed our redemption in the Glorious Descent of the Holy Spirit.

Our Father...

1: Hail Mary...
Jesus, we ask You to send us Your Holy Spirit to enlighten us in our understanding of these mysteries of our redemption;
Holy Mary...

2. Hail Mary...
Jesus in the mystery of the Nativity, we pray for the spiritual fruit of poverty of spirit;
Holy Mary...

3. Hail Mary...
Jesus in the mystery of the Nativity, we pray for the spiritual fruit of understanding;
Holy Mary...

4. Hail Mary...
Jesus in the mystery of Your proclamation of the Gospels, we pray for the spiritual fruit of evangelization;
Holy Mary...

5. Hail Mary...
Jesus in the mystery of Your proclamation of the Gospels, we pray for the spiritual fruit of prudence and zeal;
Holy Mary...

6. Hail Mary...
 Jesus in the mystery of the Crowning with Thorns, we pray
 for the spiritual fruit of mortification of our thoughts;
 Holy Mary...

7. Hail Mary...
 Jesus in the mystery of the Crowning with Thorns, we
 pray for the spiritual fruit of mortification of foolish Pride;
 Holy Mary...

8. Hail Mary...
 Jesus in the mystery of the Descent of the Holy Spirit, we
 pray for the spiritual fruit of new life in the Spirit;
 Holy Mary...

9. Hail Mary...
 Jesus in the mystery of the Descent of the Holy Spirit, we
 pray for the spiritual fruit of His anointing;
 Holy Mary...

10. Hail Mary...
 Jesus, we ask You for an increase in the gifts of the Holy
 Spirit: that we may come to know You clearer, follow You
 nearer, and love You dearer;
 Holy Mary...

Glory be...

Oh my Jesus...

THE FOURTH SACRED MYSTERIES OF THE ROSARY OF OUR REDEMPTION

The joy of the Presentation was illuminated by Your Transfiguration. You ransomed us through the sorrow and shedding of Your blood during the Carrying of the Cross and revealed our redemption in the Glorious Assumption of Your Blessed Mother into heaven.

Our Father...

1. Hail Mary...
Jesus, we ask You to send us Your Holy Spirit to enlighten us in our understanding of these mysteries of our redemption;
Holy Mary...

2. Hail Mary...
Jesus in the mystery of the Presentation, we pray for the spiritual fruit of purity of mind and body;
Holy Mary...

3. Hail Mary...
Jesus in the mystery of the Presentation, we pray for the spiritual fruit of being Jesus to others;
Holy Mary...

4. Hail Mary...
Jesus in the mystery of Your Transfiguration, we pray for the spiritual fruit of listening to God's beloved Son;
Holy Mary...

5. Hail Mary...
Jesus in the mystery of Your Transfiguration, we pray for the spiritual fruit of courage;
Holy Mary...

6. Hail Mary...

Jesus in the mystery of the Carrying of the Cross, we pray for the spiritual fruit of patience;

Holy Mary...

7. Hail Mary...

Jesus in the mystery of the Carrying of the Cross, we pray for the spiritual fruit of perseverance;

Holy Mary...

8. Hail Mary...

Jesus in the mystery of the Assumption of Your Blessed Mother into heaven, we pray for the spiritual fruit of our Blessed Mother's intercession;

Holy Mary...

9. Hail Mary...

Jesus in the mystery of the Assumption of Your Blessed Mother into heaven, we pray for the spiritual fruit of going to Jesus through Mary;

Holy Mary...

10. Hail Mary...

Jesus, we ask You for an increase in the gifts of the Holy Spirit: that we may come to know You clearer, follow You nearer, and love You dearer;

Holy Mary...

Glory be...

Oh my Jesus...

NEW DAY

IS DAWNING

THE FIFTH
SACRED MYSTERIES
OF THE ROSARY OF OUR
REDEMPTION

The joy of Finding the Child Jesus in the Temple was illuminated by Your Institution of the Eucharist. You ransomed us through the sorrow and shedding of Your blood in the Crucifixion and revealed our redemption in the Glorious Coronation of Your Blessed Mother as Queen of Heaven and Earth.

Our Father...

1. Hail Mary...

Jesus, we ask You to send us Your Holy Spirit to enlighten us in our understanding of these mysteries of our redemption;

Holy Mary...

2. Hail Mary...

Jesus in the mystery of Finding the Child Jesus in the Temple, we pray for the spiritual fruit of doing the Father's will;

Holy Mary...

3. Hail Mary...

Jesus in the mystery of Finding the Child Jesus in the Temple, we pray for the spiritual fruit of being the Temple of God;

Holy Mary...

4. Hail Mary...

Jesus in the mystery of Your Institution of the Eucharist, we pray for the spiritual fruit of loving our Eucharistic Lord;

Holy Mary...

5. Hail Mary...

Jesus in the mystery of Your Institution of the Eucharist, we pray for the spiritual fruit of daily communion;

Holy Mary...

6. Hail Mary...

Jesus in the mystery of the Crucifixion, we pray for the spiritual fruit of His Divine Mercy;

Holy Mary...

7. **Hail Mary...**
   Jesus in the mystery of the Crucifixion, we pray for the spiritual fruit of total surrender and perseverance;
   Holy Mary...

8. **Hail Mary...**
   Jesus in the mystery of the Coronation of Your Blessed Mother as Queen of Heaven and Earth, we pray for the spiritual fruit of His amazing grace;
   Holy Mary...

9. **Hail Mary...**
   Jesus in the mystery of the Coronation of Your Blessed Mother as Queen of Heaven and Earth, we pray for the spiritual fruit of a deep love of our Blessed Mother;
   Holy Mary...

10. **Hail Mary...**
    Jesus, we ask You for an increase in the gifts of the Holy Spirit: that we may come to know You clearer, follow You nearer, and love You dearer;
    Holy Mary...

Glory be...

Oh my Jesus...

   Hail, Holy Queen... (pg. 5)

   Let us pray. Oh God, whose only begotten Son... (pg. 4)

   St. Michael the Archangel... (pg. 5)

   For the intentions of the Holy Father:

   Our Father...

   Hail Mary...

   Glory be...

   In the beginning was the Word... (pg. 209)

THE TIMELESS DIVINE MERCY ROSARY

The Timeless Divine Mercy Rosary blends the traditional prayers of the Rosary, viewed in a timeless way, with the Divine Mercy Prayer given by God to Saint Faustina. It will draw down God's mercy on us and the whole world.

This Rosary can be prayed when others ask us for our prayers or when we feel the burden of the world's sinfulness weighing us down, as it did our Lord during His agony in the garden. It was here that He asked us to watch and pray with Him for an hour. Jesus promised unimaginable graces to those souls who trust in His mercy and say this prayer (*Diary of Saint Maria Faustina Kowalska*, 687). When we pray the Divine Mercy Rosary, we are going to Jesus, with our Blessed Mother's intercession, to pray for His Divine Mercy on all souls.

1. Lovely Lady dressed in blue... (pg. 1)

2. Come, Holy Spirit... (pg. 2)

3. Hail bright star of ocean... (pg. 3)

4. Let us pray. Oh God, whose only begotten Son... (pg. 4)

5. (Sign of the Cross)
   In the name of the Father...

I Believe in God... (Apostles' Creed, pg. 4)

Our Father...

Hail Mary...
Jesus, we ask You for an increase in the gift of Faith:
(Hebrews 11:1-3, 6, pg. 6)
Holy Mary...

Hail Mary...
Jesus, we ask You for an increase in the gift of Hope:
(Romans 8:14-28, pg. 6)
Holy Mary...

Hail Mary...
Jesus, we ask You for an increase in the gift of Love:
(1 Corinthians 13:1-13, pg. 7)
Holy Mary...

Glory be...

Oh my Jesus... (Fatima Prayer, pg. 5)

You expired, Jesus, but the source of life gushed forth for souls, and the ocean of mercy opened up for the whole world.

Oh Fountain of Life, unfathomable Divine Mercy, envelop the whole world and empty Yourself upon us (*Diary*, 1319).

Pray three times:
Oh Blood and Water which gushed forth from the heart of Jesus as a fountain of mercy for us, I trust in You (*Diary*, 73).

N.B.: The prayer intention suggested in the brackets for the following mysteries is optional.
e.g. {The souls in Purgatory and the unborn}.
Feel free to use this or another prayer intention, as the Spirit moves you, where the brackets indicate.

THE FIRST SACRED MYSTERIES OF THE ROSARY OF OUR REDEMPTION

The joy of the Annunciation was illuminated by Your Baptism. You ransomed us through the sorrow and shedding of Your blood during the Agony in the Garden and revealed our redemption in Your Glorious Resurrection.

Our Father...

Eternal Father, we offer You the Body, Blood, Soul, and Divinity of Your dearly beloved Son, our Lord Jesus Christ, in atonement for our sins and those of the whole world.

Father, for the sake of His sorrowful passion, have mercy on us and on the whole world. {The souls in Purgatory and the unborn}

1. Hail Mary...

Jesus, we ask You to send us Your Holy Spirit to enlighten us in our understanding of these mysteries of our redemption;
Holy Mary...

2. Hail Mary...

Jesus in the mystery of the Annunciation; Father, for the sake of His sorrowful passion, have mercy on us and on the whole world; {The souls in Purgatory and the unborn}
Holy Mary...

3. Hail Mary...

Jesus in the mystery of the Annunciation; Father, for the sake of His sorrowful passion, have mercy on us and on the whole world; {The souls in Purgatory and the unborn}
Holy Mary...

4. Hail Mary...

Jesus in the mystery of Your Baptism; Father, for the sake of His sorrowful passion, have mercy on us and on the whole world; {The souls in Purgatory and the unborn}
Holy Mary...

5. Hail Mary...

Jesus in the mystery of Your Baptism; Father, for the sake of His sorrowful passion, have mercy on us and on the whole world; {The souls in Purgatory and the unborn}
Holy Mary...

6. Hail Mary...

Jesus in the mystery of the Agony in the Garden; Father, for the sake of His sorrowful passion, have mercy on us and on the whole world; {The souls in Purgatory and the unborn}

Holy Mary...

7. Hail Mary...

Jesus in the mystery of the Agony in the Garden; Father, for the sake of His sorrowful passion, have mercy on us and on the whole world; {The souls in Purgatory and the unborn}

Holy Mary...

8. Hail Mary...

Jesus in the mystery of Your Resurrection; Father, for the sake of His sorrowful passion, have mercy on us and on the whole world; {The souls in Purgatory and the unborn}

Holy Mary...

9. Hail Mary...

Jesus in the mystery of Your Resurrection; Father, for the sake of His sorrowful passion, have mercy on us and on the whole world; {The souls in Purgatory and the unborn}

Holy Mary...

10. Hail Mary...

Jesus; Father, for the sake of His sorrowful passion, have mercy on us and on the whole world, {The souls in Purgatory and the unborn} and we ask You for an increase in the gifts of the Holy Spirit: that we may come to know You clearer, follow You nearer, and love You dearer;

Holy Mary...

Glory be...

Oh my Jesus...

THE SECOND
SACRED MYSTERIES
OF THE ROSARY OF OUR
REDEMPTION

The joy of the Visitation was illuminated by Your miracle at the Wedding Feast of Cana. You ransomed us through the sorrow and shedding of Your blood during the Scourging at the Pillar and revealed our redemption in Your Glorious Ascension.

Our Father...

Eternal Father, we offer You the Body, Blood, Soul, and Divinity of Your dearly beloved Son our Lord Jesus Christ in atonement for our sins and those of the whole world.

Father, for the sake of His sorrowful passion, have mercy on us and on the whole world. {The souls in Purgatory and the unborn}

1. Hail Mary...

Jesus, we ask You to send us Your Holy Spirit to enlighten us in our understanding of these mysteries of our redemption; **Holy Mary...**

2. Hail Mary...

Jesus in the mystery of the Visitation; Father, for the sake of His sorrowful passion, have mercy on us and on the whole world; {The souls in Purgatory and the unborn} **Holy Mary...**

3. Hail Mary...

Jesus in the mystery of the Visitation; Father, for the sake of His sorrowful passion, have mercy on us and on the whole world; {The souls in Purgatory and the unborn} **Holy Mary...**

4. Hail Mary...

Jesus in the mystery of the Wedding Feast at Cana; Father, for the sake of His sorrowful passion, have mercy on us and on the whole world; {The souls in Purgatory and the unborn} **Holy Mary...**

5.Hail Mary...

Jesus in the mystery of the Wedding Feast at Cana; Father, for the sake of His sorrowful passion, have mercy on us and on the whole world; {The souls in Purgatory and the unborn} **Holy Mary...**

6. Hail Mary...

Jesus in the mystery of the Scourging at the Pillar; Father, for the sake of His sorrowful passion, have mercy on us and on the whole world; {The souls in Purgatory and the unborn}

Holy Mary...

7. Hail Mary...

Jesus in the mystery of the Scourging at the Pillar; Father, for the sake of His sorrowful passion, have mercy on us and on the whole world; {The souls in Purgatory and the unborn}

Holy Mary...

8. Hail Mary...

Jesus in the mystery of Your Ascension; Father, for the sake of His sorrowful passion, have mercy on us and on the whole world; {The souls in Purgatory and the unborn}

Holy Mary...

9. Hail Mary...

Jesus in the mystery of Your Ascension; Father, for the sake of His sorrowful passion, have mercy on us and on the whole world; {The souls in Purgatory and the unborn}

Holy Mary...

10. Hail Mary...

Jesus; Father, for the sake of His sorrowful passion, have mercy on us and on the whole world, {The souls in Purgatory and the unborn} and we ask You for an increase in the gifts of the Holy Spirit: that we may come to know You clearer, follow You nearer, and love You dearer;

Holy Mary...

Glory be...

Oh my Jesus...

THE THIRD SACRED MYSTERIES OF THE ROSARY OF OUR REDEMPTION

The joy of the Nativity was illuminated by Your proclamation of the Gospels. You ransomed us through the sorrow and shedding of Your blood during the Crowning with Thorns and revealed our redemption in the Glorious Descent of the Holy Spirit.

Our Father...

Eternal Father, we offer You the Body, Blood, Soul, and Divinity of Your dearly beloved Son our Lord Jesus Christ in atonement for our sins and those of the whole world.

Father, for the sake of His sorrowful passion, have mercy on us and on the whole world. {The souls in Purgatory and the unborn}

1. Hail Mary...

Jesus, we ask You to send us Your Holy Spirit to enlighten us in our understanding of these mysteries of our redemption; **Holy Mary...**

2. Hail Mary...

Jesus in the mystery of the Nativity; Father, for the sake of His sorrowful passion, have mercy on us and on the whole world; {The souls in Purgatory and the unborn} **Holy Mary...**

3. Hail Mary...

Jesus in the mystery of the Nativity; Father, for the sake of His sorrowful passion, have mercy on us and on the whole world; {The souls in Purgatory and the unborn} **Holy Mary...**

4. Hail Mary...

Jesus in the mystery of Your proclamation of the Gospels; Father, for the sake of His sorrowful passion, have mercy on us and on the whole world; {The souls in Purgatory and the unborn} **Holy Mary...**

5. Hail Mary...

Jesus in the mystery of Your proclamation of the Gospels; Father, for the sake of His sorrowful passion, have mercy on us and on the whole world; {The souls in Purgatory and the unborn} **Holy Mary...**

6. Hail Mary...

Jesus in the mystery of the Crowning with Thorns; Father, for the sake of His sorrowful passion, have mercy on us and on the whole world; {The souls in Purgatory and the unborn}
Holy Mary...

7. Hail Mary...

Jesus in the mystery of the Crowning with Thorns; Father, for the sake of His sorrowful passion, have mercy on us and on the whole world; {The souls in Purgatory and the unborn}
Holy Mary...

8. Hail Mary...

Jesus in the mystery of the Descent of the Holy Spirit; Father, for the sake of His sorrowful passion, have mercy on us and on the whole world; {The souls in Purgatory and the unborn}
Holy Mary...

9. Hail Mary...

Jesus in the mystery of the Descent of the Holy Spirit; Father, for the sake of His sorrowful passion, have mercy on us and on the whole world; {The souls in Purgatory and the unborn}
Holy Mary...

10. Hail Mary...

Jesus; Father, for the sake of His sorrowful passion, have mercy on us and on the whole world, {The souls in Purgatory and the unborn} and we ask You for an increase in the gifts of the Holy Spirit: that we may come to know You clearer, follow You nearer, and love You dearer;
Holy Mary...

Glory be...

Oh my Jesus...

THE FOURTH SACRED MYSTERIES OF THE ROSARY OF OUR REDEMPTION

The joy of the Presentation was illuminated by Your Transfiguration. You ransomed us through the sorrow and shedding of Your blood during the Carrying of the Cross and revealed our redemption in the Glorious Assumption of Your Blessed Mother into heaven.

Our Father...

Eternal Father, we offer You the Body, Blood, Soul, and Divinity of Your dearly beloved Son our Lord Jesus Christ in atonement for our sins and those of the whole world.

Father, for the sake of His sorrowful passion, have mercy on us and on the whole world. {The souls in Purgatory and the unborn}

1. Hail Mary...

Jesus, we ask You to send us Your Holy Spirit to enlighten us in our understanding of these mysteries of our redemption;
Holy Mary...

2. Hail Mary...

Jesus in the mystery of the Presentation; Father, for the sake of His sorrowful passion, have mercy on us and on the whole world; {The souls in Purgatory and the unborn}
Holy Mary...

3. Hail Mary...

Jesus in the mystery of the Presentation; Father, for the sake of His sorrowful passion, have mercy on us and on the whole world; {The souls in Purgatory and the unborn}
Holy Mary...

4. Hail Mary...

Jesus in the mystery of Your Transfiguration; Father, for the sake of His sorrowful passion, have mercy on us and on the whole world; {The souls in Purgatory and the unborn}
Holy Mary...

5. Hail Mary...

Jesus in the mystery of Your Transfiguration; Father, for the sake of His sorrowful passion, have mercy on us and on the whole world; {The souls in Purgatory and the unborn}
Holy Mary...

6. Hail Mary...

Jesus in the mystery of the Carrying of the Cross; Father, for the sake of His sorrowful passion, have mercy on us and on the whole world; {The souls in Purgatory and the unborn}
Holy Mary...

7. Hail Mary...

Jesus in the mystery of the Carrying of the Cross; Father, for the sake of His sorrowful passion, have mercy on us and on the whole world; {The souls in Purgatory and the unborn}
Holy Mary...

8. Hail Mary...

Jesus in the mystery of the Assumption of Your Blessed Mother into heaven; Father, for the sake of His sorrowful passion, have mercy on us and on the whole world; {The souls in Purgatory and the unborn}
Holy Mary...

9. Hail Mary...

Jesus in the mystery of the Assumption of Your Blessed Mother into heaven; Father, for the sake of His sorrowful passion, have mercy on us and on the whole world;{The souls in Purgatory and the unborn}
Holy Mary...

10. Hail Mary...

Jesus; Father, for the sake of His sorrowful passion, have mercy on us and on the whole world, {The souls in Purgatory and the unborn} and we ask You for an increase in the gifts of the Holy Spirit: that we may come to know You clearer, follow You nearer, and love You dearer;
Holy Mary...

Glory be...

Oh my Jesus...

NEW DAY

IS DAWNING

The Fifth
Sacred Mysteries
of the Rosary of our
Redemption

The joy of Finding the Child Jesus in the Temple was illuminated by Your Institution of the Eucharist. You ransomed us through the sorrow and shedding of Your blood in the Crucifixion and revealed our redemption in the Glorious Coronation of Your Blessed Mother as Queen of Heaven and Earth.

Our Father...

Eternal Father, we offer You the Body, Blood, Soul, and Divinity of Your dearly beloved Son our Lord Jesus Christ in atonement for our sins and those of the whole world. Father, for the sake of His sorrowful passion, have mercy on us and on the whole world. {The souls in Purgatory and the unborn}

1. Hail Mary...

Jesus, we ask You to send us Your Holy Spirit to enlighten us in our understanding of these mysteries of our redemption;
Holy Mary...

2. Hail Mary...

Jesus in the mystery of Finding the Child Jesus in the Temple; Father, for the sake of His sorrowful passion, have mercy on us and on the whole world; {The souls in Purgatory and the unborn}
Holy Mary...

3. Hail Mary...

Jesus in the mystery of Finding the Child Jesus in the Temple; Father, for the sake of His sorrowful passion, have mercy on us and on the whole world; {The souls in Purgatory and the unborn}
Holy Mary...

4. Hail Mary...

Jesus in the mystery of Your Institution of the Eucharist; Father, for the sake of His sorrowful passion, have mercy on us and on the whole world; {The souls in Purgatory and the unborn}
Holy Mary...

5. Hail Mary...

Jesus in the mystery of Your Institution of the Eucharist; Father, for the sake of His sorrowful passion, have mercy on us and on the whole world; {The souls in Purgatory and the unborn}
Holy Mary...

6. Hail Mary...

Jesus in the mystery of Your Crucifixion; Father, for the sake of His sorrowful passion, have mercy on us and on the whole world; {The souls in Purgatory and the unborn} **Holy Mary...**

7. Hail Mary...

Jesus in the mystery of Your Crucifixion; Father, for the sake of His sorrowful passion, have mercy on us and on the whole world; {The souls in Purgatory and the unborn} **Holy Mary...**

8. Hail Mary...

Jesus in the mystery of the Coronation of Your Blessed Mother as Queen of Heaven and Earth; Father, for the sake of His sorrowful passion, have mercy on us and on the whole world; {The souls in Purgatory and the unborn} **Holy Mary...**

9. Hail Mary...

Jesus in the mystery of the Coronation of Your Blessed Mother as Queen of Heaven and Earth; Father, for the sake of His sorrowful passion, have mercy on us and on the whole world; {The souls in Purgatory and the unborn} **Holy Mary...**

10. Hail Mary...

Jesus; Father, for the sake of His sorrowful passion, have mercy on us and on the whole world, {The souls in Purgatory and the unborn}and we ask You for an increase in the gifts of the Holy Spirit: that we may come to know You clearer, follow You nearer, and love You dearer; **Holy Mary...**

Glory be...

Oh my Jesus...

Hail, Holy Queen... (pg. 5)

Let us pray. Oh God, whose only begotten Son... (pg. 4)

St. Michael the Archangel... (pg. 5)

For the intentions of the Holy Father:

> **Our Father...**
>
> **Hail Mary...**
>
> **Glory be...**

In the beginning was the Word... (pg. 209)

Eternal God, in whom mercy is endless and the treasury of compassion is inexhaustible, look kindly upon us and increase Your mercy upon us, that in difficult moments we might not despair nor become despondent, but with great confidence submit ourselves to Your holy will, which is Love and Mercy itself (*Diary*, 950).

Jesus, I trust in You.

Jesus, I trust in You.

Jesus, I trust in You.

THE TIMELESS PENITENTIAL ROSARY

The Timeless Penitential Rosary blends the traditional prayers of the Rosary, viewed in a timeless way, with the 51st Psalm. This lets you walk alongside King David as he pleads with God for mercy while acknowledging his own sinfulness. The rosary consists of eight petitions, all of which King David prayed when his sinfulness was discovered and brought to light by Nathan, the Prophet.

This Rosary is best prayed with a humble and contrite heart after a fall from grace. With the help of the Holy Spirit and sacramental confession, if available, lost grace can quickly be restored while your will is strengthened to battle future temptations.

1. Lovely Lady dressed in blue... (pg. 1)

2. Come, Holy Spirit... (pg. 2)

3. Hail bright star of ocean... (pg. 3)

4. Let us pray. Oh God, whose only begotten Son... (pg. 4)

5. (Sign of the Cross) In the name of the Father...

I Believe in God... (Apostles' Creed, pg. 4)

Our Father...

Hail Mary...
Jesus, we ask You for an increase in the gift of Faith:
(Hebrews 11:1-3, 6, pg. 6)
Holy Mary...

Hail Mary...
Jesus, we ask You for an increase in the gift of Hope:
(Romans 8:14-28, pg. 6)
Holy Mary...

Hail Mary...
Jesus, we ask You for an increase in the gift of Love:
(1 Corinthians 13:1-13, pg. 7)
Holy Mary...

Glory be...

Oh my Jesus... (Fatima Prayer, pg. 5)

Act of Contrition:

Oh my God I am heartily sorry for having offended You. And I detest all my sins, because I dread the loss of heaven and the pains of hell, but most of all because I have offended You, Oh my God, Who art all good and deserving of all of my love. I firmly resolve, with the help Thy grace, to confess my sins, to do penance, and to amend my life. Amen.

The First Sacred Mysteries of the Rosary of our Redemption

The joy of the Annunciation was illuminated by Your Baptism. You ransomed us through the sorrow and shedding of Your blood during the Agony in the Garden and revealed our redemption in Your Glorious Resurrection.

Our Father...

1. Hail Mary...

Jesus, we ask You to send us Your Holy Spirit to enlighten us in our understanding of these mysteries of our redemption;
Holy Mary...

2. Hail Mary...

Jesus in the mystery of the Annunciation we pray: Psalm 51:3-4, [3]Have mercy on me, Oh God, in your goodness; in your abundant compassion blot out my offense. [4]Wash away all my guilt; from my sin cleanse me;
Holy Mary...

3. Hail Mary...

Jesus in the mystery of the Annunciation we pray: Psalm 51:5-6, [5]For I know my offense; as my sin is always before me. [6]Against you alone have I sinned; and done what is evil in your sight That you are just in your sentence, blameless if you condemn me;
Holy Mary...

4. Hail Mary...

Jesus in the mystery of Your Baptism we pray: Psalm 51:7-8, [7]Truly, I was conceived, a sinner. [8]Still, you consider the sincerity of my heart; in my inmost being teach me your wisdom;
Holy Mary...

5. Hail Mary...

Jesus in the mystery of Your Baptism we pray: Psalm 51:9-10, [9]Cleanse me with hyssop, that I may be pure; wash me, make me whiter than snow. [10]Let me hear again the sounds of joy and gladness; let the bones you have crushed be renewed;
Holy Mary...

6. Hail Mary...

Jesus in the mystery of the Agony in the Garden we pray: Psalm 51:11-12, [11]Turn away your face from my sins; blot out all my guilt. [12]A clean heart create for me, Oh God; renew in me a steadfast spirit;

Holy Mary...

7. Hail Mary...

Jesus in the mystery of the Agony in the Garden we pray: Psalm 51:13-15, [13]Do not drive me from your presence, nor take from me your Holy Spirit [14]Restore my joy in your salvation; sustain in me a willing spirit. [15]Help me to teach the wicked your ways, that sinners may return to you;

Holy Mary...

8. Hail Mary...

Jesus in the mystery of Your Resurrection we pray: Psalm 51:16-18, [16]Rescue me from death, Oh God, my saving God, that my tongue may praise your healing power. [17]Lord, open my lips; and let my mouth proclaim your praise. [18]For you do not desire sacrifice; a burnt offering you would not accept;

Holy Mary...

9. Hail Mary...

Jesus in the mystery of Your Resurrection we pray: Psalm 51:19-20, [19]My sacrifice, Oh God, is a broken spirit; Oh God, You will not spurn a broken, contrite and humbled heart. [20]Let Zion again prosper in your good pleasure; rebuild the walls of Jerusalem. Then you will be pleased with proper sacrifice, of Holy hands lifted to You in praise;

Holy Mary...

10. Hail Mary...

Jesus, we ask You for an increase in the gifts of the Holy Spirit: that we may come to know You clearer, follow You nearer, and love You dearer;

Holy Mary...

Glory be...

Oh my Jesus...

THE SECOND SACRED MYSTERIES OF THE ROSARY OF OUR REDEMPTION

The joy of the Visitation was illuminated by Your miracle at the Wedding Feast of Cana. You ransomed us through the sorrow and shedding of Your blood during the Scourging at the Pillar and revealed our redemption in Your Glorious Ascension.

Our Father...

1. Hail Mary...

Jesus, we ask You to send us Your Holy Spirit to enlighten us in our understanding of these mysteries of our redemption;
Holy Mary...

2. Hail Mary...

Jesus in the mystery of the Visitation we pray: Psalm 51:3-4, [3]Have mercy on me, Oh God, in your goodness; in your abundant compassion blot out my offense. [4]Wash away all my guilt; from my sin cleanse me;
Holy Mary...

3. Hail Mary...

Jesus in the mystery of the Visitation we pray: Psalm 51:5-6, [5]For I know my offense; as my sin is always before me. [6]Against you alone have I sinned; and done what is evil in your sight That you are just in your sentence, blameless if you condemn me;
Holy Mary...

4. Hail Mary...

Jesus in the mystery of the Wedding Feast at Cana we pray: Psalm 51:7-8, [7]Truly, I was conceived, a sinner. [8]Still, you consider the sincerity of my heart; in my inmost being teach me your wisdom;
Holy Mary...

5. Hail Mary...

Jesus in the mystery of the Wedding Feast at Cana we pray: Psalm 51:9-10, [9]Cleanse me with hyssop, that I may be pure; wash me, make me whiter than snow. [10]Let me hear again the sounds of joy and gladness; let the bones you have crushed be renewed;
Holy Mary...

6. Hail Mary...

Jesus in the mystery of the Scourging at the Pillar we pray: Psalm 51:11-12, [11]Turn away your face from my sins; blot out all my guilt. [12]A clean heart create for me, Oh God; renew in me a steadfast spirit;

Holy Mary...

7. Hail Mary...

Jesus in the mystery of the Scourging at the Pillar we pray: Psalm 51:13-15, [13]Do not drive me from your presence, nor take from me your Holy Spirit [14]Restore my joy in your salvation; sustain in me a willing spirit. [15]Help me to teach the wicked your ways, that sinners may return to you;

Holy Mary...

8. Hail Mary...

Jesus in the mystery of Your Ascension we pray: Psalm 51:16-18, [16]Rescue me from death, Oh God, my saving God, that my tongue may praise your healing power. [17]Lord, open my lips; and let my mouth proclaim your praise. [18]For you do not desire sacrifice; a burnt offering you would not accept;

Holy Mary...

9. Hail Mary...

Jesus in the mystery of Your Ascension we pray: Psalm 51:19-20, [19]My sacrifice, Oh God, is a broken spirit; Oh God, You will not spurn a broken, contrite and humbled heart. [20]Let Zion again prosper in your good pleasure; rebuild the walls of Jerusalem. Then you will be pleased with proper sacrifice, of Holy hands lifted to You in praise;

Holy Mary...

10. Hail Mary...

Jesus, we ask You for an increase in the gifts of the Holy Spirit: that we may come to know You clearer, follow You nearer, and love You dearer;

Holy Mary...

Glory be...

Oh my Jesus...

THE THIRD SACRED MYSTERIES OF THE ROSARY OF OUR REDEMPTION

The joy of the Nativity was illuminated by Your proclamation of the Gospels. You ransomed us through the sorrow and shedding of Your blood during the Crowning with Thorns and revealed our redemption in the Glorious Descent of the Holy Spirit.

Our Father...

1. Hail Mary...

Jesus, we ask You to send us Your Holy Spirit to enlighten us in our understanding of these mysteries of our redemption;

Holy Mary...

2. Hail Mary...

Jesus in the mystery of the Nativity we pray: Psalm 51:3-4, [3]Have mercy on me, Oh God, in your goodness; in your abundant compassion blot out my offense. [4]Wash away all my guilt; from my sin cleanse me;

Holy Mary...

3. Hail Mary...

Jesus in the mystery of the Nativity we pray: Psalm 51:5-6, [5]For I know my offense; as my sin is always before me. [6]Against you alone have I sinned; and done what is evil in your sight That you are just in your sentence, blameless if you condemn me;

Holy Mary...

4. Hail Mary...

Jesus in the mystery of Your proclamation of the Gospels we pray: Psalm 51:7-8, [7]Truly, I was conceived, a sinner. [8]Still, you consider the sincerity of my heart; in my inmost being teach me your wisdom;

Holy Mary...

5. Hail Mary...

Jesus in the mystery of Your proclamation of the Gospels we pray: Psalm 51:9-10, [9]Cleanse me with hyssop, that I may be pure; wash me, make me whiter than snow. [10]Let me hear again the sounds of joy and gladness; let the bones you have crushed be renewed;

Holy Mary...

6. Hail Mary...

Jesus in the mystery of the Crowning with Thorns we pray: Psalm 51:11-12, [11]Turn away your face from my sins; blot out all my guilt. [12]A clean heart create for me, Oh God; renew in me a steadfast spirit;

Holy Mary...

7. Hail Mary...

Jesus in the mystery of the Crowning with Thorns we pray: Psalm 51:13-15, [13]Do not drive me from your presence, nor take from me your Holy Spirit [14]Restore my joy in your salvation; sustain in me a willing spirit. [15]Help me to teach the wicked your ways, that sinners may return to you;

Holy Mary...

8. Hail Mary...

Jesus in the mystery of the Descent of the Holy Spirit we pray: Psalm 51:16-18, [16]Rescue me from death, Oh God, my saving God, that my tongue may praise your healing power. [17]Lord, open my lips; and let my mouth proclaim your praise. [18]For you do not desire sacrifice; a burnt offering you would not accept;

Holy Mary...

9. Hail Mary...

Jesus in the mystery of the Descent of the Holy Spirit we pray: Psalm 51:19-20, [19]My sacrifice, Oh God, is a broken spirit; Oh God, You will not spurn a broken, contrite and humbled heart. [20]Let Zion again prosper in your good pleasure; rebuild the walls of Jerusalem. Then you will be pleased with proper sacrifice, of Holy hands lifted to You in praise;

Holy Mary...

10. Hail Mary...

Jesus, we ask You for an increase in the gifts of the Holy Spirit: that we may come to know You clearer, follow You nearer, and love You dearer;

Holy Mary...

Glory be...

Oh my Jesus...

The Fourth Sacred Mysteries of the Rosary of our Redemption

The joy of the Presentation was illuminated by Your Transfiguration. You ransomed us through the sorrow and shedding of Your blood during the Carrying of the Cross and revealed our redemption in the Glorious Assumption of Your Blessed Mother into heaven.

Our Father...

1. Hail Mary...

Jesus, we ask You to send us Your Holy Spirit to enlighten us in our understanding of these mysteries of our redemption;

Holy Mary...

2. Hail Mary...

Jesus in the mystery of the Presentation we pray: Psalm 51:3-4, [3]Have mercy on me, Oh God, in your goodness; in your abundant compassion blot out my offense. [4]Wash away all my guilt; from my sin cleanse me;

Holy Mary...

3. Hail Mary...

Jesus in the mystery of the Presentation we pray: Psalm 51:5-6, [5]For I know my offense; as my sin is always before me. [6]Against you alone have I sinned; and done what is evil in your sight That you are just in your sentence, blameless if you condemn me;

Holy Mary...

4. Hail Mary...

Jesus in the mystery of Your Transfiguration we pray: Psalm 51:7-8, [7]Truly, I was conceived, a sinner. [8]Still, you consider the sincerity of my heart; in my inmost being teach me your wisdom;

Holy Mary...

5. Hail Mary...

Jesus in the mystery of Your Transfiguration we pray: Psalm 51:9-10, [9]Cleanse me with hyssop, that I may be pure; wash me, make me whiter than snow. [10]Let me hear again the sounds of joy and gladness; let the bones you have crushed be renewed;

Holy Mary...

6. Hail Mary...

Jesus in the mystery of the Carrying of the Cross we pray: Psalm 51:11-12, [11]Turn away your face from my sins; blot out all my guilt. [12]A clean heart create for me, Oh God; renew in me a steadfast spirit;

Holy Mary...

7. Hail Mary...

Jesus in the mystery of the Carrying of the Cross we pray: Psalm 51:13-15, [13]Do not drive me from your presence, nor take from me your Holy Spirit [14]Restore my joy in your salvation; sustain in me a willing spirit. [15]Help me to teach the wicked your ways, that sinners may return to you;

Holy Mary...

8. Hail Mary...

Jesus in the mystery of the Assumption of Your Blessed Mother into heaven we pray: Psalm 51:16-18, [16]Rescue me from death, Oh God, my saving God, that my tongue may praise your healing power. [17]Lord, open my lips; and let my mouth proclaim your praise. [18]For you do not desire sacrifice; a burnt offering you would not accept;

Holy Mary...

9. Hail Mary...

Jesus in the mystery of the Assumption of Your Blessed Mother into heaven we pray: Psalm 51:19-20, [19]My sacrifice, Oh God, is a broken spirit; Oh God, You will not spurn a broken, contrite and humbled heart. [20]Let Zion again prosper in your good pleasure; rebuild the walls of Jerusalem. Then you will be pleased with proper sacrifice, of Holy hands lifted to You in praise;

Holy Mary...

10. Hail Mary...

Jesus, we ask You for an increase in the gifts of the Holy Spirit: that we may come to know You clearer, follow You nearer, and love You dearer;

Holy Mary...

Glory be...

Oh my Jesus...

NEW DAY

IS DAWNING

The Fifth
Sacred Mysteries
of the Rosary of our
Redemption

The joy of Finding the Child Jesus in the Temple was illuminated by Your Institution of the Eucharist. You ransomed us through the sorrow and shedding of Your blood in the Crucifixion and revealed our redemption in the Glorious Coronation of Your Blessed Mother as Queen of Heaven and Earth.

Our Father...

1. Hail Mary...
Jesus, we ask You to send us Your Holy Spirit to enlighten us in our understanding of these mysteries of our redemption;
Holy Mary...

2. Hail Mary...
Jesus in the mystery of Finding the Child Jesus in the Temple we pray: Psalm 51:3-4, [3]Have mercy on me, Oh God, in your goodness; in your abundant compassion blot out my offense. [4]Wash away all my guilt; from my sin cleanse me;
Holy Mary...

3. Hail Mary...
Jesus in the mystery of Finding the Child Jesus in the Temple we pray: Psalm 51:5-6, [5]For I know my offense; as my sin is always before me. [6]Against you alone have I sinned; and done what is evil in your sight That you are just in your sentence, blameless if you condemn me;
Holy Mary...

4. Hail Mary...
Jesus in the mystery of Your Institution of the Eucharist we pray: Psalm 51:7-8, [7]Truly, I was conceived, a sinner. [8]Still, you consider the sincerity of my heart; in my inmost being teach me your wisdom;
Holy Mary...

5. Hail Mary...
Jesus in the mystery of Your Institution of the Eucharist we pray: Psalm 51:9-10, [9]Cleanse me with hyssop, that I may be pure; wash me, make me whiter than snow. [10]Let me hear again the sounds of joy and gladness; let the bones you have crushed be renewed;
Holy Mary...

6. Hail Mary...
Jesus in the mystery of the Crucifixion we pray: Psalm 51:11-12, [11]Turn away your face from my sins; blot out all my guilt. [12]A clean

heart create for me, Oh God; renew in me a steadfast spirit;
Holy Mary...

7. Hail Mary...

Jesus in the mystery of the Crucifixion we pray: Psalm 51:13-15, [13]Do not drive me from your presence, nor take from me your Holy Spirit [14]Restore my joy in your salvation; sustain in me a willing spirit. [15]Help me to teach the wicked your ways, that sinners may return to you;
Holy Mary...

8. Hail Mary...

Jesus in the mystery of the Coronation of Your Blessed Mother as Queen of Heaven and Earth we pray: Psalm 51:16-18, [16]Rescue me from death, Oh God, my saving God, that my tongue may praise your healing power. [17]Lord, open my lips; and let my mouth proclaim your praise. [18]For you do not desire sacrifice; a burnt offering you would not accept;
Holy Mary...

9. Hail Mary...

Jesus in the mystery of the Coronation of Your Blessed Mother as Queen of Heaven and Earth we pray: Psalm 51:19-20, [19]My sacrifice, Oh God, is a broken spirit; Oh God, You will not spurn a broken, contrite and humbled heart. [20]Let Zion again prosper in your good pleasure; rebuild the walls of Jerusalem. Then you will be pleased with proper sacrifice, of Holy hands lifted to You in praise;
Holy Mary...

10. Hail Mary...

Jesus, we ask You for an increase in the gifts of the Holy Spirit: that we may come to know You clearer, follow You nearer, and love You dearer;
Holy Mary...

Glory be...

Oh my Jesus...

Hail, Holy Queen... (pg. 5)

Let us pray. Oh God, whose only begotten Son...
(pg. 4)

St. Michael the Archangel... (pg. 5)

For the intentions of the Holy Father:

  Our Father...

  Hail Mary...

  Glory be...

In the beginning was the Word... (pg. 209)

THE TIMELESS SCRIPTURAL ROSARY

The Timeless Scriptural Rosary blends the traditional prayers of the Rosary, viewed in a timeless way, with extensive study of the Sacred Scripture verses which correspond to the mystery being prayed. This helps to paint a universally historic, literal, yet prophetic picture of our salvation. We do this by asking our Lord to send us His Holy Spirit to accompany us on our Scriptural meditative journey through the mysteries of our redemption. We will ask before starting this journey that He open up our minds and hearts, just as He did to the disciples on the road to Emmaus.

This Rosary can be prayed when making a Holy Hour, as it can be very intense and may cause you to lose track of the time you spent with The Timeless One. However, you may find yourself saying at the end of an intimate Holy Hour, as did the disciples on the road to Emmaus, "Stay with us, Lord, for the day is far spent." You will always finish filled with joy and a better knowledge of His great Love for you. Hopefully you will want to share this joy with others.

Rosary Reflections

1. **Lovely Lady dressed in blue...** (pg. 1)

2. **Come, Holy Spirit...** (pg. 2)

3. **Hail bright star of ocean...** (pg. 3)

4. **Let us pray. Oh God, whose only begotten Son...** (pg. 4)

5. (Sign of the Cross)
   In the name of the Father...

I Believe in God... (Apostles' Creed, pg. 4)

Our Father...

Hail Mary...
Jesus, we ask You for an increase in the gift of Faith:
(Hebrews 11:1-3, 6, pg. 6)
Holy Mary...

Hail Mary...
Jesus, we ask You for an increase in the gift of Hope:
(Romans 8:14-28, pg. 6)
Holy Mary...

Hail Mary...
Jesus, we ask You for an increase in the gift of Love:
(1 Corinthians 13:1-13, pg. 7)
Holy Mary...

Glory be...

Oh my Jesus... (Fatima Prayer, pg. 5)

The First
Sacred Mysteries
of the Rosary of our
Redemption

The joy of the Annunciation was illuminated by Your Baptism. You ransomed us through the sorrow and shedding of Your blood during the Agony in the Garden and revealed our redemption in Your Glorious Resurrection.

Rosary Reflections

Our Father...

1. Hail Mary...

Jesus, we ask You to send us Your Holy Spirit to enlighten us in our understanding of these mysteries of our redemption;

Holy Mary...

2. Luke 1:26-33 Hail Mary...

Jesus in the mystery of the Annunciation. [26]In the sixth month, the angel Gabriel was sent from God to a town of Galilee called Nazareth, [27]to a virgin betrothed to a man named Joseph, of the house of David, and the virgin's name was Mary. [28]And coming to her, he said, "Hail, favored one! The Lord is with you." [29]But she was greatly troubled at what was said and pondered what sort of greeting this might be. [30]Then the angel said to her, "Do not be afraid, Mary, for you have found favor with God. [31]Behold, you will conceive in your womb and bear a son, and you shall name him Jesus. [32]He will be great and will be called Son of the Most High, and the Lord God will give him the throne of David his father, [33]and he will rule over the house of Jacob forever, and of his kingdom there will be no end."

Holy Mary...

3. Luke 1:34-38 Hail Mary...

Jesus in the mystery of the Annunciation. [34]But Mary said to the angel, "How can this be, since I have no relations with a man?" [35]And the angel said to her in reply, "The Holy Spirit will come upon you, and the power of the Most High will overshadow you. Therefore the child to be born will be called holy, the Son of God. [36]And behold, Elizabeth, your relative, has also conceived a son in her old age, and this is the sixth month for her who was called barren; [37]for nothing will be impossible for God." [38]Mary

said, "Behold, I am the handmaid of the Lord. May it be done to me according to your word." Then the angel departed from her.
Holy Mary.

4. Matthew 3:1-2, 11-15 Hail Mary...

Jesus in the mystery of Your Baptism. [1]In those days, John the Baptist, appeared preaching in the desert of Judea and [2]saying "Repent, for the kingdom of heaven is at hand! [11]I am baptizing you with water, for repentance, but the one who is coming after me is mightier than I. I am not worthy to carry his sandals. He will baptize you with the Holy Spirit and fire. [12]His winnowing fan is in his hand. He will clear his threshing floor and gather his wheat into his barn, but the chaff he will burn with unquenchable fire." [13]Then Jesus came from Galilee to John at the Jordan to be baptized by him. [14]John tried to prevent him, saying, "I need to be baptized by you, and yet you are coming to me?" [15]Jesus said to him in reply, "Allow it now, for thus it is fitting for us to fulfill all righteousness."
Holy Mary...

5. Mark 1:7-13 Hail Mary...

Jesus in the mystery of Your Baptism. [7]And this is what John proclaimed: "One mightier than I is coming after me. I am not worthy to stoop and loosen the thongs of his sandals. [8]I have baptized you with water; he will baptize you with the Holy Spirit." [9]It happened in those days that Jesus came from Nazareth of Galilee and was baptized in the Jordan by John. [10]on coming up out of the water he saw the heavens being torn open and the Spirit, like a dove, descending upon him. [11]And a voice came from the heavens, "You are my beloved Son; with you I am well pleased."
Holy Mary...

6. Matthew 26:36-41 Hail Mary...

Jesus in the mystery of the Agony in the Garden. [36]Then Jesus came with them to a place called Gethsemane, and he said to his disciples, "Sit here while I go over there and pray." [37]He took along Peter and the two sons of Zebedee, and began to feel sorrow and distress. [38]Then he said to them, "My soul is sorrowful even to death. Remain here and keep watch with me." [39]He advanced a little and fell prostrate in prayer, saying, "My Father, if it is possible, let this cup pass from me; yet, not as I will, but as you will." [40]When he returned to his disciples he found them asleep. He said to Peter, "So you could not keep watch with me for one hour? [41]Watch and pray that you may not undergo the test. The spirit is willing, but the flesh is weak."

Holy Mary...

7. Mark 14:39-41 Hail Mary...

Jesus in the mystery of the Agony in the Garden. [39]Withdrawing again, he prayed, saying the same thing. [40]Then he returned once more and found them asleep, for they could not keep their eyes open and did not know what to answer him. [41]He returned a third time and said to them, "Are you still sleeping and taking your rest? It is enough. The hour has come. Behold, the Son of Man is to be handed over to sinners.

Holy Mary...

8. Matthew 28:5-8 Hail Mary...

Jesus in the mystery of Your Resurrection. [5]Then the angel said to the women in reply, "Do not be afraid! I know that you are seeking Jesus the crucified. [6]He is not here, for he has been raised just as he said. Come and see the place where he lay. [7]Then go quickly and tell his disciples, 'He has been raised from the dead, and he is going before you to Galilee; there you will see him.' Behold, I have told you." [8]Then they went away quickly from the tomb, fearful yet overjoyed, and ran to announce this to his disciples.

Holy Mary...

9. Luke 24:13-35 Hail Mary...

Jesus in the mystery of Your Resurrection. [13]Now that very day two of them who were going to a village seven miles from Jerusalem called Emmaus, [14]and they were conversing about all the things that had occurred. [15]And it happened that while they were conversing and debating, Jesus himself drew near and walked with them, [16]but their eyes were prevented from recognizing him. [17]He asked them, "What are you discussing as you walk along?" They stopped, looking downcast. [18]One of them, named Cleopas, said to him in reply, "Are you the only visitor to Jerusalem who does not know of the things that have taken place there in these days?" [19]And he replied to them, "What sort of things?" They said to him, "The things that happened to Jesus the Nazarene, who was a prophet mighty in deed and word before God and all the people, [20]how our chief priests and rulers both handed him over to a sentence of death and crucified him. [21]But we were hoping that he would be the one to redeem Israel; and besides all this, it is now the third day since this took place. [22]Some women from our group, however, have astounded us: they were at the tomb early in the morning [23]and did not find his body; they came back and reported that they had indeed seen a vision of angels who announced that he was alive. [24]Then some of those with us went to the tomb and found things just as the women had described, but him they did not see." [25]And he said to them, "Oh, how foolish you are! How slow of heart to believe all that the prophets spoke! [26]Was it not necessary that the Messiah should suffer these things and enter into his glory?" [27]Then beginning with Moses and all the prophets, he interpreted to them what referred to him in all the scriptures. [28]As they approached the village to which they were going, he gave the impression that he was going on farther. ²⁹But they urged him, "Stay with us, for it is nearly evening and the day is almost over." So he went in to stay with them. ³⁰And it happened that, while he was with them at table, he took bread, said the blessing, broke it, and gave it to them. ³¹With that their eyes were opened and they recognized him, but he vanished from their sight. ³²Then they said to each other, "Were not our hearts burning within us while he spoke to us on the way and opened the scriptures to us?" ³³So they set out at once and returned to Jerusalem where they found gathered together the eleven and those with them ³⁴who were saying, "The Lord has truly been raised and has appeared to Simon!" ³⁵Then the two recounted what had taken place on the way and how he was made known to them in the breaking of the bread.

Holy Mary...

10. Hail Mary...

Jesus, we ask You for an increase in the gifts of the Holy Spirit: that we may come to know You clearer, follow You nearer, and love You dearer;

Holy Mary...

Glory be...

Oh my Jesus...

THE SECOND
SACRED MYSTERIES
OF THE ROSARY OF OUR
REDEMPTION

The joy of the Visitation was illuminated by Your miracle at the Wedding Feast of Cana. You ransomed us through the sorrow and shedding of Your blood during the Scourging at the Pillar and revealed our redemption in Your Glorious Ascension.

Rosary Reflections

Our Father...

1. Hail Mary...
Jesus, we ask You to send us Your Holy Spirit to enlighten us in our understanding of these mysteries of our redemption;
Holy Mary...

2. Luke 1:39-45 Hail Mary...
Jesus in the mystery of the Visitation. [39]During those days Mary set out and traveled to the hill country in haste to a town of Judah, [40]where she entered the house of Zechariah and greeted Elizabeth. [41]When Elizabeth heard Mary's greeting, the infant leaped in her womb, and Elizabeth, filled with the Holy Spirit, [42]cried out in a loud voice and said, "Most blessed are you among women, and blessed is the fruit of your womb. [43]And how does this happen to me, that the mother of my Lord should come to me? [44]For at the moment the sound of your greeting reached my ears, the infant in my womb leaped for joy. [45]Blessed are you who believed that what was spoken to you by the Lord would be fulfilled."
Holy Mary...

3. Luke 1:46-56 Hail Mary...
Jesus in the mystery of the Visitation [46]Mary said: "My soul proclaims the greatness of the Lord; [47]my spirit rejoices in God my savior. [48]for he has looked upon his handmaid's lowliness; behold, from now on will all ages call me blessed. [49]The Mighty One has done great things for me, and holy is his name. [50]His mercy is from age to age to those who fear him. [51]He has shown might with his arm, dispersed the arrogant of mind and heart. [52]He has thrown down the rulers from their thrones but lifted up the lowly. [53]The hungry he has filled with good things; the rich he has sent away empty. [54]He has helped Israel

his servant, remembering his mercy, [55]according to his promise to our fathers, to Abraham and to his descendants forever." [56]Mary remained with her about three months and then returned to her home.

Holy Mary...

4. John 2:1-4 Hail Mary...

Jesus in the mystery of the Wedding Feast at Cana. [1]On the third day there was a wedding in Cana in Galilee, and the mother of Jesus was there. [2]Jesus and his disciples were also invited to the wedding. [3]When the wine ran short, the mother of Jesus said to him, "They have no wine." [4]And Jesus said to her, "Woman, how does your concern affect me? My hour has not yet come." [5]His mother said to the servers, "Do whatever he tells you." [6]Now there were six stone water jars there for Jewish ceremonial washings, each holding twenty to thirty gallons. [7]Jesus told them, "Fill the jars with water." So they filled them to the brim. [8]Then he told them, "Draw some out now and take it to the headwaiter." So they took it.

Holy Mary...

5. John 2:9-12 Hail Mary...

Jesus in the mystery of the Wedding Feast at Cana. [9]And when the headwaiter tasted the water that had become wine, without knowing where it came from although the servers who had drawn the water knew, the headwaiter called the bridegroom [10]and said to him, "Everyone serves good wine first, and then when people have drunk freely, an inferior one; but you have kept the good wine until now." [11]Jesus did this as the beginning of his signs in Cana in Galilee and so revealed his glory, and his disciples began to believe in him. [12]After this, he and his mother, his brothers, and his disciples went down to Capernaum and stayed there only a few days.

Holy Mary..

6. John 18:33-40, 19:1 Hail Mary...

Jesus in the mystery of the Scourging at the Pillar. [33] Pilate went back into the praetorium and summoned Jesus and said to him, "Are you the King of the Jews?" [34]Jesus answered, "Do you say this on your own or have others told you about me?" [35]Pilate answered, "I am not a Jew, am I? Your own nation and the chief priests handed you over to me. What have you done?" [36]Jesus answered, "My kingdom does not belong to this world. If my kingdom did belong to this world, my attendants would be fighting to keep me from being handed over to the Jews. But as it is, my kingdom is not here." [37]So Pilate said to him, "Then you are a king?" Jesus answered, "You say I am a king. For this I was born and for this I came into the world, to testify to the truth. Everyone who belongs to the truth listens to my voice." [38]Pilate said to him, "What is truth?" When he had said this, he again went out to the Jews and said to them, "I find no guilt in him. [39]But you have a custom that I release one prisoner to you at Passover. Do you want me to release to you the King of the Jews?" [40]They cried out again, "Not this one but Barabbas!" Now Barabbas was a revolutionary. [1]Then Pilate took Jesus and had him scourged.

Holy Mary...

7. Matthew 27:15-26 Hail Mary...

Jesus in the mystery of the Scourging at the Pillar. [15]Now on the occasion of the feast the governor was accustomed to release to the crowd one prisoner whom they wished. [16]And at that time they had a notorious prisoner called Barabbas. [17]So when they had assembled, Pilate said to them, "Which one do you want me to release to you, Barabbas, or Jesus called Messiah?" [18]For he knew that it was out of envy that they had handed Him over. [19]While he was still seated on the bench, his wife sent him a message, "Have nothing to do with that righteous man. I suffered much in a dream today because of him." [20]The chief priests and the elders persuaded the crowds to ask for Barabbas but to destroy Jesus. [21]The governor said to them in reply, "Which of the two do you want me to release to you?" They answered, "Barabbas!" [22]Pilate said to them, "Then what shall I do with Jesus called Messiah?" They all said, "Let him be crucified!" [23]But he said, "Why? What evil has he done?" They only shouted the louder, "Let him be crucified!" [24]When Pilate saw that he was not succeeding at all, but that a riot was breaking out instead, he took water and washed his hands in the sight of the crowd, saying, "I am innocent of this man's blood. Look to it yourselves." [25]And the whole people said in reply, "His blood be upon us and upon our children." [26]Then he released Barabbas to them, but after he had Jesus scourged, he handed him over to be crucified.

Holy Mary...

8. Matthew 28:16-20 Hail Mary...

Jesus in the mystery of Your Ascension. [16]The eleven disciples went to Galilee, to the mountain to which He had ordered them. [17]When they saw him, they worshiped, but they doubted. [18]Then Jesus approached and said to them, "All power in heaven and on earth has been given to me. [19]Go, therefore, and make disciples of all nations, baptizing them in the name of the Father, and of the Son, and of the Holy Spirit, [20]teaching them to observe all that I have commanded you. And behold, I am with you always, until the end of the age."

Holy Mary...

9. Acts 1:4-11 Hail Mary...

Jesus in the mystery of Your Ascension. [4]Jesus had enjoined them not to depart from Jerusalem, but to wait for "the promise of the Father about which you have heard me speak; [5]for John baptized with water, but in a few days you will be baptized with the Holy Spirit." ⁶When they had gathered together they asked him, "Lord, are you at this time going to restore the kingdom to Israel?" ⁷He answered them, "It is not for you to know the times or seasons that the Father has established by his own authority. ⁸But you will receive power when the Holy Spirit comes upon you, and you will be my witnesses in Jerusalem, throughout Judea and Samaria, and to the ends of the earth." ⁹When he had said this, as they were looking on, he was lifted up, and a cloud took him from their sight. ¹⁰While they were looking intently at the sky as he was going, suddenly two men dressed in white garments stood beside them. ¹¹They said, "Men of Galilee, why are you standing there looking at the sky? This Jesus who has been taken up from you into heaven will return in the same way as you have seen him going into heaven."

Holy Mary...

10. Hail Mary...

Jesus, we ask You for an increase in the gifts of the Holy Spirit: that we may come to know You clearer, follow You nearer, and love You dearer;

Holy Mary...

Glory be...

Oh my Jesus...

THE THIRD
SACRED MYSTERIES
OF THE ROSARY OF OUR
REDEMPTION

The joy of the Nativity was illuminated by Your proclamation of the Gospels. You ransomed us through the sorrow and shedding of Your blood during the Crowning with Thorns and revealed our redemption in the Glorious Descent of the Holy Spirit.

Our Father...

1. Hail Mary...

Jesus, we ask You to send us Your Holy Spirit to enlighten us in our understanding of these mysteries of our redemption; **Holy Mary...**

2. Matthew 1:18, 20-24 Hail Mary...

Jesus in the mystery of the Nativity. [18]When, behold, the angel of the Lord appeared to him in a dream and said, "Joseph, son of David, do not be afraid to take Mary your wife into your home. For it is through the Holy Spirit that this child has been conceived in her. [21]She will bear a son and you are to name him Jesus, because he will save his people from their sins." [22]All this took place to fulfill what the Lord had said through the prophet: [23] "Behold, the virgin shall be with child and bear a son, and they shall name him Emmanuel," which means "God is with us." [24] When Joseph awoke, he did as the angel of the Lord had commanded him and took his wife into his home.

Holy Mary...

3. Matthew 2:1-2, 9-12 Hail Mary...

Jesus in the mystery of the Nativity. [1]When Jesus was born in Bethlehem of Judea, in the days of King Herod, behold, magi from the east arrived in Jerusalem, [2]saying, "Where is the newborn king of the Jews? We saw his star at its rising and have come to do him homage." [9]After their audience with the king they set out. And behold, the star that they had seen at its rising preceded them, until it came and stopped over the place where the child was. [10]They were overjoyed at seeing the star, [11]and on entering the house they saw the child with Mary his mother. They prostrated themselves and did him homage. Then they opened their treasures and offered him gifts of gold, frankincense, and myrrh. [12]And having been warned in a dream not to return to Herod, they departed for their country by another way.

Holy Mary...

4. Matthew 5:1-12 Hail Mary...

Jesus in the mystery of Your proclamation of the Gospels. ¹When he saw the crowds, he went up the mountain, and after he had sat down, his disciples came to him. ²He began to teach them, saying: ³Blessed are the poor in spirit, for theirs is the kingdom of heaven. ⁴Blessed are they who mourn, for they will be comforted. ⁵Blessed are the meek, for they will inherit the land. ⁶Blessed are they who hunger and thirst for righteousness, they will be satisfied. ⁷Blessed are the merciful, for they will be shown mercy. ⁸Blessed are the clean of heart, for they will see God. ⁹Blessed are the peacemakers, for they will be called children of God. ¹⁰Blessed are they who are persecuted for the sake of righteousness, for theirs is the kingdom of heaven. ¹¹Blessed are you when they insult you and persecute you and utter every kind of evil against you falsely because of me. ¹²Rejoice and be glad, for your reward will be great in heaven. Thus they persecuted the prophets who were before you.

Holy Mary...

5. Matthew 6:25-34 Hail Mary...

Jesus in the mystery of Your proclamation of the Gospels. ²⁵"Therefore I tell you, do not worry about your life, what you will eat or drink, or about your body, what you will wear. Is not life more than food and the body more than clothing? ²⁶Look at the birds in the sky; they do not sow or reap, they gather nothing into barns, yet your heavenly Father feeds them. Are not you more important than they? ²⁷Can any of you by worrying add a single moment to your life-span? ²⁸Why are you anxious about clothes? Learn from the way the wild flowers grow. They do not work or spin. ²⁹But I tell you that not even Solomon in his entire splendor was clothed like one of them. ³⁰If God so clothes the grass of the field, which grows today and is thrown into the oven tomorrow, will he not much more provide for you, O you of little faith? ³¹So do not worry

and say, 'What are we to eat?' or 'What are we to drink?' or 'What are we to wear?' [32]All these things the pagans seek. Your heavenly Father knows that you need them all. [33]But seek first the kingdom of God and his righteousness and all these things will be given you besides. [34]Do not worry about tomorrow; tomorrow will take care of itself. Sufficient for a day is its own evil.
Holy Mary...

6. John 19:1-5 Hail Mary...

Jesus in the mystery of the Crowning with Thorns. [1]Pilate took and had him scourged. [2]And the soldiers wove a crown out of thorns and placed it on his head, and clothed him in a purple cloak, [3]and they came to him and said, "Hail, King of the Jews!" And they struck him repeatedly. [4]Once more Pilate went out and said to them, "Look, I am bringing him out to you, so that you may know that I find no guilt in him." [5]So Jesus came out, wearing the crown of thorns and the purple cloak. And he said to them, "Behold, the man!"
Holy Mary...

7. Matthew 27:27-31 Hail Mary...

Jesus in the mystery of the Crowning with Thorns. [27]Then the soldiers of the governor took Jesus inside the praetorium and gathered the whole cohort around him. [28]They stripped off his clothes and threw a scarlet military cloak about him. [29]Weaving a crown out of thorns, they placed it on his head, and a reed in his right hand. And kneeling before him, they mocked him, saying, "Hail, King of the Jews!" [30]They spat upon him and took the reed and kept striking him on the head. [31]And when they had mocked him, they stripped him of the cloak, dressed him in his own clothes, and led him off to crucify him.
Holy Mary...

8. Acts 2:1-4 Hail Mary...

Jesus in the mystery of the Descent of the Holy Spirit.

¹When the time for Pentecost was fulfilled, they were all in one place together. ²And suddenly there came from the sky a noise like a strong driving wind, and it filled the entire house in which they were. ³Then there appeared to them tongues as of fire, which parted and came to rest on each one of them. ⁴And they were all filled with the Holy Spirit and began to speak in different tongues, as the Spirit led them to proclaim.
Holy Mary...

9. Acts 2:5-12 Hail Mary...
Jesus in the mystery of the Descent of the Holy Spirit. ⁵Now there were devout Jews from every nation under heaven staying in Jerusalem. ⁶At this sound, they gathered in a large crowd, but they were confused because each one heard them speaking in his own language. ⁷They were astounded, and in amazement they asked, "Are not all these people who are speaking Galileans? ⁸Then how does each of us hear them in his own native language? ⁹We are Parthians, Medes, and Elamites, inhabitants of Mesopotamia, Judea and Cappadocia, Pontus and Asia, ¹⁰Phrygia and Pamphylia, Egypt and the districts of Libya near Cyrene, as well as travelers from Rome, ¹¹both Jews and converts to Judaism, Cretans and Arabs, yet we hear them speaking in our own tongues of the mighty acts of God." ¹²They were all astounded and bewildered, and said to one another, "What does this mean?"
Holy Mary...

10. Hail Mary...
Jesus, we ask You for an increase in the gifts of the Holy Spirit: that we may come to know You clearer, follow You nearer, and love You dearer;
Holy Mary...

Glory be...

Oh my Jesus...

THE FOURTH
SACRED MYSTERIES
OF THE ROSARY OF OUR
REDEMPTION

The joy of the Presentation was illuminated by Your Transfiguration. You ransomed us through the sorrow and shedding of Your blood during the Carrying of the Cross and revealed our redemption in the Glorious Assumption of Your Blessed Mother into heaven.

Rosary Reflections

Our Father...

1. Hail Mary...
    Jesus, we ask You to send us Your Holy Spirit to enlighten us in our understanding of these mysteries of our redemption;
    Holy Mary...

2. Luke 2:21-23 Hail Mary...
    Jesus in the mystery of the Presentation. [21] When eight days were completed for his circumcision; He was named Jesus, the name given him by the angel before he was conceived in the womb. [22] When the days were completed for their purification according to the law of Moses, they took him up to Jerusalem to present him to the Lord, [23] just as it is written in the law of the Lord, "Every male that opens the womb shall be consecrated to the Lord,"
    Holy Mary...

3. Luke 2:25-35 Hail Mary...
    Jesus in the mystery of the Presentation. [25]Now there was a man in Jerusalem whose name was Simeon. This man was righteous and devout, awaiting the consolation of Israel, and the Holy Spirit was upon him. [26]It had been revealed to him by the Holy Spirit that he should not see death before he had seen the Messiah of the Lord. [27]He came in the Spirit into the temple; and when the parents brought in the child Jesus to perform the custom of the law in regard to him, [28]he took him into his arms and blessed God, saying: [29]"Now, Master, you may let your servant go in peace, according to your word, [30]for my eyes have seen your salvation, [31]which you prepared in sight of all the peoples, [32]a light for revelation to the Gentiles, and glory for your people Israel." [33]The child's father and mother were amazed at what was said about him; [34]and Simeon blessed them and said to Mary his mother, "Behold, this child is destined for the fall and rise of many in Israel, and

to be a sign that will be contradicted [35]and you yourself a sword will pierce so that the thoughts of many hearts may be revealed."

Holy Mary...

4. Luke 9:23-36 Hail Mary...

Jesus in the mystery of Your Transfiguration. [23]Then he said to all, "If anyone wishes to come after me, he must deny himself and take up his cross daily and follow me. [24]For whoever wishes to save his life will lose it, but whoever loses his life for my sake will save it. [25]What profit is there for one to gain the whole world yet lose or forfeit himself? [26]Whoever is ashamed of me and of my words, the Son of Man will be ashamed of when he comes in his glory and in the glory of the Father and of the holy angels. [27]Truly I say to you, there are some standing here who will not taste death until they see the kingdom of God." [28]About eight days after he said this, he took Peter, John, and James and went up the mountain to pray. [29]While he was praying his face changed in appearance and his clothing became dazzling white. [30]And behold, two men were conversing with him, Moses and Elijah, [31]who appeared in glory and spoke of his exodus that he was going to accomplish in Jerusalem. [32]Peter and his companions had been overcome by sleep, but becoming fully awake, they saw his glory and the two men standing with him. [33]As they were about to part from him, Peter said to Jesus, "Master, it is good that we are here; let us make three tents, one for you, one for Moses, and one for Elijah." But he did not know what he was saying. [34]While he was still speaking, a cloud came and cast a shadow over them, and they became frightened when they entered the cloud. [35]Then from the cloud came a voice that said, "This is my chosen Son; listen to him." [36]After the voice had spoken, Jesus was found alone. They fell silent and did not at that time tell anyone what they had seen.

Holy Mary...

5. Matthew 17:9-13   Hail Mary...

Jesus in the mystery of Your Transfiguration. [9]As they were coming down from the mountain, Jesus charged them, "Do not tell the vision to anyone until the Son of Man has been raised from the dead." [10]Then the disciples asked him, "Why do the scribes say that Elijah must come first?" [11]He said in reply, "Elijah will indeed come and restore all things; [12]but I tell you that Elijah has already come, and they did not recognize him but did to him whatever they pleased. So also will the Son of Man suffer at their hands." [13]Then the disciples understood that he was speaking to them of John the Baptist.

Holy Mary...

6. Matthew 27:32-35   Hail Mary...

Jesus in the mystery of the Carrying of the Cross. [32]As they were going out, they met a Cyrenian named Simon; this man they pressed into service to carry his cross. [33]And when they came to a place called Golgotha which means Place of the Skull, [34]they gave Jesus wine to drink mixed with gall. But when he had tasted it, he refused to drink. [35]After they had crucified him, they divided his garments by casting lots.

Holy Mary...

7. Luke 23:26-31   Hail Mary...

Jesus in the mystery of the Carrying of the Cross. [26]When they led him away they took hold of a certain Simon, a Cyrenian, who was coming in from the country; and after laying the cross on him, they made him carry it behind Jesus. [27]A large crowd of people followed Jesus, including many women who mourned and lamented him. [28]Jesus turned to them and said, "Daughters of Jerusalem, do not weep for me; weep instead for yourselves and for your children, [29]for indeed, the days are coming when people will say, 'Blessed are the barren, the wombs that never bore and the breasts that never nursed.' [30]At that time people

will say to the mountains, 'Fall upon us!' and to the hills, 'Cover us!' [31]for if these things are done when the wood is green what will happen when it is dry?"
Holy Mary...

8. Isaiah 54:1-10 Hail Mary...

Jesus in the mystery of the Assumption of Your Blessed Mother into heaven. [1]Raise a glad cry, you barren one who did not bear, break forth in jubilant song, you who were not in labor, For more numerous are the children of the deserted wife than the children of her who has a husband, says the Lord. [2]Enlarge the space for your tent, spread out your tent cloths unsparingly; lengthen your ropes and make firm your stakes. [3]For you shall spread abroad to the right and to the left; Your descendants shall dispossess the nations and shall inhabit the desolate cities.

[4]Fear not, you shall not be put to shame; you need not blush, for you shall not be disgraced. The shame of your youth you shall forget, the reproach of your widowhood no longer remember. [5]For he who has become your husband is your Maker; his name is the Lord of hosts; Your redeemer is the Holy One of Israel, called God of all the earth. [6]The Lord calls you back, like a wife forsaken and grieved in spirit, A wife married in youth and then cast off, says your God. [7]For a brief moment I abandoned you, but with great tenderness I will take you back. [8]In an outburst of wrath, for a moment I hid my face from you; But with enduring love I take pity on you, says the Lord, your redeemer. [9]This is for me like the days of Noah, when I swore that the waters of Noah should never again deluge the earth; So I have sworn not to be angry with you, or to rebuke you. [10]Though the mountains leave their place and the hills be shaken, My love shall never leave you nor my covenant of peace be shaken, says the LORD, who has mercy on you.
Holy Mary...

9. Zephaniah 3:14-20 Hail Mary...

Jesus in the mystery of the Assumption of Your Blessed Mother into heaven. [14]Shout for joy, O daughter Zion! sing joyfully, O Israel! Be glad and exult with all your heart, O daughter Jerusalem! [15]The LORD has removed the judgment against you, he has turned away your enemies; The King of Israel, the LORD, is in your midst, you have no further misfortune to fear. [16]On that day, it shall be said to Jerusalem: Fear not, O Zion, be not discouraged! [17]The LORD, your God, is in your midst, a mighty savior; He will rejoice over you with gladness, and renew you in his love, He will sing joyfully because of you, [18]as one sings at festivals. I will remove disaster from among you, so that none may recount your disgrace. [19]Yes, at that time I will deal with all who oppress you; I will save the lame, and assemble the outcasts; I will give them praise and renown in all the earth, when I bring about their restoration. [20]At that time I will bring you home, and at that time I will gather you; For I will give you renown and praise, among all the peoples of the earth, When I bring about your restoration before our very eyes, says the Lord.

Holy Mary...

10. Hail Mary...

Jesus, we ask You for an increase in the gifts of the Holy Spirit: that we may come to know You clearer, follow You nearer, and love You dearer;

Holy Mary...

Glory be...

Oh my Jesus...

THE FIFTH
SACRED MYSTERIES
OF THE ROSARY OF OUR
REDEMPTION

The joy of Finding the Child Jesus in the Temple was illuminated by Your Institution of the Eucharist. You ransomed us through the sorrow and shedding of Your blood in the Crucifixion and revealed our redemption in the Glorious Coronation of Your Blessed Mother as Queen of Heaven and Earth.

Our Father...

1. Hail Mary...
Jesus, we ask You to send us Your Holy Spirit to enlighten us in our understanding of these mysteries of our redemption;
Holy Mary...

2. Luke 2:41-47 Hail Mary...
Jesus in the mystery of Finding the Child Jesus in the Temple. [41]Each year his parents went to Jerusalem for the feast of Passover, [42]and when he was twelve years old, they went up according to festival custom. [43]After they had completed its days, as they were returning, the boy Jesus remained behind in Jerusalem, but his parents did not know it. [44]Thinking that he was in the caravan, they journeyed for a day and looked for him among their relatives and acquaintances, [45]but not finding him, they returned to Jerusalem to look for him. [46]After three days they found him in the temple, sitting in the midst of the teachers, listening to them and asking them questions, [47]and all who heard him, were astounded at his understanding and his answers.
Holy Mary...

3. Luke 2:48-49 Hail Mary...
Jesus in the mystery of Finding the Child Jesus in the Temple. [48]When his parents saw him, they were astonished, and his mother said to him, "Son, why have you done this to us? Your father and I have been looking for you with great anxiety." [49]And he said to them, "Why were you looking for me? Did you not know that I must be in my Father's house?"
Holy Mary...

4. Matthew 26:26-29 Hail Mary...
Jesus in the mystery of Your Institution of the Eucharist. [26]While they were eating, Jesus took bread, said the blessing, broke it, and giving it to his disciples said, "Take and eat; this is my body." [27]Then he took a cup, gave thanks, and

gave it to them, saying, "Drink from it, all of you, [28]for this is my blood of the covenant, which will be shed on behalf of many for the forgiveness of sins. [29]I tell you; from now on I shall not drink this fruit of the vine until the day when I drink it with you new in the kingdom of my Father."
Holy Mary...

5. John 6:47-58 Hail Mary...

Jesus in the mystery of Your Institution of the Eucharist. [47]Amen, amen, I say to you, whoever believes has eternal life. [48]I am the bread of life. [49]Your ancestors ate the manna in the desert, but they died; [50]this is the bread that comes down from heaven so that one may eat it and not die. [51]I am the living bread that came down from heaven; whoever eats this bread will live forever; and the bread that I will give is my flesh for the life of the world." [52]The Jews quarreled among themselves, saying, "How can this man give us his flesh to eat?" [53]Jesus said to them, "Amen, amen, I say to you, unless you eat the flesh of the Son of Man and drink his blood, you do not have life within you. [54]Whoever eats my flesh and drinks my blood has eternal life, and I will raise him on the last day. [55]For my flesh is true food and my blood is true drink. [56]Whoever eats my flesh and drinks my blood remains in me and I in him. [57]Just as the living Father sent me and I have life because of the Father, so also the one who feeds on me will have life because of me. [58]This is the bread that came down from heaven. Unlike your ancestors who ate and still died, whoever eats this bread will live forever."
Holy Mary...

6. Matthew 27:46-54 Hail Mary...

Jesus in the mystery of the Crucifixion. [46]And about three o'clock Jesus cried out in a loud voice, "Eli, Eli, lema sabachthani?" which means, "My God, my God, why have you forsaken me?" [47]Some of the bystanders who heard it said,

"This one is calling for Elijah." [48]Immediately one of them ran to get a sponge; he soaked it in wine, and putting it on a reed, gave it to him to drink. [49]But the rest said, "Wait, let us see if Elijah comes to save him." [50]But Jesus cried out again in a loud voice, and gave up his spirit. [51]And behold, the veil of the sanctuary was torn in two from top to bottom. The earth quaked, rocks were split, [52]tombs were opened, and the bodies of many saints who had fallen asleep were raised. [53]And coming forth from their tombs after his resurrection, they entered the holy city and appeared to many. [54]The centurion and the men with him who were keeping watch over Jesus feared greatly when they saw the earthquake and all that was happening, and they said, "Truly, this was the Son of God!"

Mark 15:42-46 [42]When it was already evening, since it was the day of preparation, the day before the Sabbath, [43]Joseph of Arimathea, a distinguished member of the council, who was himself awaiting the kingdom of God, came and courageously went to Pilate and asked for the body of Jesus. [44]Pilate was amazed that he was already dead. He summoned the centurion and asked him if Jesus had already died. [45]And when he learned of it from the centurion, he gave the body to Joseph. [46]Having bought a linen cloth, he took him down, wrapped him in the linen cloth and laid him in a tomb that had been hewn out of the rock. Then he rolled a stone against the entrance to the tomb.

Holy Mary...

7. Luke 23:33-43 Hail Mary...

Jesus in the mystery of the Crucifixion. [33]When they came to the place called the Skull, they crucified him and the criminals there, one on his right, the other on his left. [34]Then Jesus said, "Father, forgive them, they know not what they do." They divided his garments by casting lots. [35]The people stood by and watched; the rulers, meanwhile, sneered at him and said, "He saved others, let him save himself if he is the chosen one, the Messiah of God." ³⁶Even the soldiers jeered at him. As they approached to offer him wine ³⁷they called out, "If you are King of the Jews, save yourself." ³⁸Above him there was an inscription that read, "This is the King of the Jews." ³⁹Now one of the criminals hanging there reviled Jesus, saying, "Are you not the Messiah? Save yourself and us." ⁴⁰The other, however, rebuking him, said in reply, "Have you no fear of God, for you are subject to the same condemnation? ⁴¹And indeed, we have been condemned justly, for the sentence we received corresponds to our crimes, but this man has done nothing criminal." ⁴²Then he said, "Jesus, remember me when you come into your kingdom." ⁴³He replied to him, "Amen, I say to you, today you will be with me in Paradise."

John 19:25-37 ²⁵Standing by the cross of Jesus were his mother and his mother's sister, Mary the wife of Clopas, and Mary of Magdala. ²⁶When Jesus saw his mother and the disciple there whom he loved, he said to his mother, "Woman, behold, your son." ²⁷Then he said to the disciple, "Behold, your mother." And from that hour the disciple took her into his home. ²⁸After this, aware that everything was now finished, in order that the scripture might be fulfilled, Jesus said, "I thirst." ²⁹There was a vessel filled with common wine. So they put a sponge soaked in wine on a sprig of hyssop and put it up to his mouth. ³⁰When Jesus had taken the wine, he said, "It is finished." And bowing his head, he handed over the spirit. ³¹Now since it was preparation day, in order that the bodies might not remain on the cross on the sabbath, for the sabbath day of that week was a solemn one, the Jews asked Pilate that their legs be broken and they be taken down. ³²So the soldiers came and broke the legs of the first and then of the other one who was crucified with Jesus. ³³But when they came to Jesus and saw that he was already dead, they did not break his legs, ³⁴but one soldier thrust his lance into his side, and immediately blood

and water flowed out. [35]An eyewitness has testified, and his testimony is true; he knows that he is speaking the truth, so that you also may come to believe. [36]For this happened so that the scripture passage might be fulfilled: "Not a bone of it will be broken." [37]And again another passage says: "They will look upon him whom they have pierced."
Holy Mary...

8. Revelation 11:19, 12:1-2 Hail Mary...

Jesus in the mystery of the Coronation of Your Blessed Mother as Queen of Heaven and Earth. [19]God's temple in heaven was opened, and the ark of his covenant could be seen in the temple. There were flashes of lightning, rumblings, and peals of thunder, an earthquake, and a violent hailstorm. [1]A great sign appeared in the sky, a woman clothed with the sun, with the moon under her feet, and on her head a crown of twelve stars. [2]She was with child and wailed aloud in pain as she labored to give birth.
Holy Mary...

9. Revelation 21:1-7, 23- Hail Mary...

Jesus in the mystery of the Coronation of Your Blessed Mother as Queen of Heaven and Earth. [1]Then I saw a new heaven and a new earth. The former heaven and the former earth had passed away, and the sea was no more. [2]I also saw the holy city, a new Jerusalem, coming down out of heaven from God, prepared as a bride adorned for her husband. [3]I heard a loud voice from the throne saying, "Behold, God's dwelling is with the human race. He will dwell with them and they will be his people and God himself will always be with them as their God. [4]He will wipe every tear from their eyes, and there shall be no more death or mourning, wailing or pain, for the old order has passed away."
[5]The one who sat on the throne said, "Behold, I make all things new." Then he said, "Write these words down, for they are trustworthy and true." [6]He said to me, "They are

accomplished. I am the Alpha and the Omega, the beginning and the end. To the thirsty I will give a gift from the spring of life-giving water. ⁷The victor will inherit these gifts, and I shall be his God, and he will be my son.

²³The city had no need of sun or moon to shine on it, for the glory of God gave it light, and its lamp was the Lamb. ²⁴The nations will walk by its light, and to it the kings of the earth will bring their treasure. ²⁵During the day its gates will never be shut, and there will be no night there. ²⁶The treasure and wealth of the nations will be brought there, ²⁷but nothing unclean will enter it, nor anyone who does abdominal things or tells lies. Only those will enter whose names are written in the Lamb's book of life.

Revelation 22:12-14, 17, 20-21 ¹²"Behold, I am coming soon. I bring with me the recompense I will give to each according to his deeds. ¹³I am the Alpha and the Omega, the first and the last, the beginning and the end." ¹⁴Blessed are they who wash their robes so as to have the right to the tree of life and enter the city through its gates. ¹⁷The Spirit and the bride say, "Come." Let the hearer say, "Come." Let the one who thirsts come forward, and the one who wants it receive the gift of life-giving water. ²⁰"Yes, I am coming soon." Amen! Come, Lord Jesus! ²¹The grace of the Lord Jesus be with all.

Holy Mary...

10. Hail Mary...
Jesus, we ask You for an increase in the gifts of the Holy Spirit: that we may come to know You clearer, follow You nearer, and love You dearer;

Holy Mary...

Glory be...

Oh my Jesus...

Hail, Holy Queen... (pg. 5)

Let us pray. Oh God, whose only begotten Son... (pg. 4)

St. Michael the Archangel... (pg. 5)

For the intentions of the Holy Father:

> **Our Father...**
>
> **Hail Mary...**
>
> **Glory be...**

In the beginning was the Word... (pg. 209)

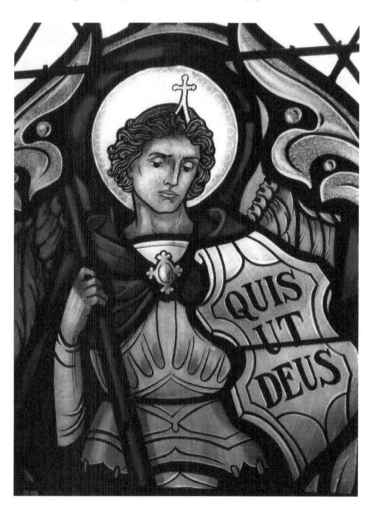

THE TIMELESS SPIRITUAL WARFARE ROSARY

The Timeless Spiritual Warfare Rosary blends the traditional prayers of the Rosary, viewed in a timeless way, with Sacred Scripture verses that correspond to the mystery being prayed, while asking our heavenly Father for His help and protection in our constant battle with sin, temptations, and other harms we may face from the world, the flesh and the Evil one. We will do this by submitting ourselves to God while resisting the Devil. We also ask our Lord to draw near and send us His Holy Spirit to protect and accompany us on our journey through this world's temptation. We will continue to pray and meditate on the wonder and love our Father has for us, in sharing His own Mother with us, and adopting us as His very own children. Once we again recognize our divine calling and remember that we are His Temple, so it will be much easier to be Holy as He is Holy.

This Rosary is best prayed as soon as we become aware of any temptation or other harm is occurring. You can even say this Rosary as a precaution against temptation even before it occurs. You will find that our Blessed Mother, her Divine Son, and our Heavenly Father are always ready to bring you the help you need to overcome any temptation or harm you may be facing. So be not afraid, start winning your spiritual battles with the help of our Blessed Mother, and her Son Who is the Captain, the Lord of Hosts and our Savior.

1. **Lovely Lady dressed in blue...** (pg. 1)

2. **Come, Holy Spirit...** (pg. 2)

3. **Hail bright star of ocean...** (pg. 3)

4. **Let us pray. Oh God, whose only begotten Son...** (pg. 4)

5. (Sign of the Cross)
   In the name of the Father...

I Believe in God... (Apostles' Creed, pg. 4)

Our Father...

Hail Mary...
Jesus, we ask You for an increase in the gift of Faith:
(Hebrews 11:1-3, 6, pg. 6)
Holy Mary...

Hail Mary...
Jesus, we ask You for an increase in the gift of Hope:
(Romans 8:14-28, pg. 6)
Holy Mary...

Hail Mary...
Jesus, we ask You for an increase in the gift of Love:
(1 Corinthians 13:1-13, pg. 7)
Holy Mary...

Glory be...

Oh my Jesus... (Fatima Prayer, pg. 5)

Psalm 91:1-16 [1]You who dwell in the shelter of the Most High, who abide in the shadow of the Almighty, [2]Say to the LORD, "My refuge and fortress, my God in whom I trust." [3]God will rescue you from the fowler's snare, from the destroying plague, [4]Will shelter you with pinions, spread wings that you may take refuge; God's faithfulness is a protecting shield. [5]You shall not fear the terror of the night nor the arrow that flies by day, [6]Nor the pestilence that roams in darkness, nor the plague that ravages at noon. [7]Though a thousand fall at your side, ten thousand at your right hand, near you it shall not come. [8]You need simply watch; the punishment of the wicked you will see. [9]You have the LORD for your refuge; you have made the Most High your stronghold. [10]No evil shall befall you, no affliction come near your tent. [11]For God commands the angels to guard you in all your ways. [12]With their hands they shall support you, lest you strike your foot against a stone. [13]You shall tread upon the asp and the viper, trample the lion and the dragon. [14]Whoever clings to me I will deliver; whoever knows my name I will set on high. [15]All who call upon me I will answer; I will be with them in distress; I will deliver them and give them honor. [16]With length of days I will satisfy them and show them my saving power.

The First
Sacred Mysteries
of the Rosary of our
Redemption

The joy of the Annunciation was illuminated by Your Baptism. You ransomed us through the sorrow and shedding of Your blood during the Agony in the Garden and revealed our redemption in Your Glorious Resurrection.

Our Father...

1. James 4:7-8 Hail Mary...

[7]So submit yourselves to God. Resist the devil, and he will flee from you. [8]Draw near to God, and he will draw near to you. We ask You to send us Your Holy Spirit to enlighten us in our understanding of these mysteries of our redemption; **Holy Mary...**

2. 1 John 3:1-3 Hail Mary...

Jesus in the mystery of the Annunciation. [1]See what love the Father has bestowed on us that we may be called the children of God. Yet so we are. The reason the world does not know us is that it did not know him. [2]Beloved, we are God's children now; what we shall be has not yet been revealed. We do know that when it is revealed we shall be like him, for we shall see him as he is. [3]Everyone who has this hope based on him makes himself pure, as he is pure. **John 2:15-17** [15]Do not love the world or the things of the world. If anyone loves the world, the love of the Father is not in him. [16] For all that is in the world, sensual lust, enticement for the eyes, and a pretentious life, is not from the Father but is from the world. [17] Yet the world and its enticement are passing away. But whoever does the will of God remains forever. **Holy Mary...**

3. Philippians 4:4-9 Hail Mary...

Jesus in the mystery of the Annunciation. [4]Rejoice in the Lord always. I shall say it again: rejoice! [5]Your kindness should be known to all. The Lord is near. [6]Have no anxiety at all, but in everything, by prayer and petition, with thanksgiving, make your requests known to God. [7]Then the peace of God that surpasses all understanding will guard your hearts and minds in Christ Jesus. [8]Finally, brothers, whatever is true, whatever is honorable, whatever is just, whatever is pure, whatever is lovely, whatever is gracious, if there is any excellence and if there is anything worthy of praise, think about these things.

⁹Keep on doing what you have learned and received and heard and seen in me. Then the God of peace will be with you.
Holy Mary.

4. Romans 6:2-7 Hail Mary...

Jesus in the mystery of Your Baptism. ²How can we who died to sin yet live in it? ³Or are you unaware that we who were baptized into Christ Jesus were baptized into his death? ⁴We were indeed buried with him through baptism into death, so that, just as Christ was raised from the dead by the glory of the Father, we too might live in newness of life. ⁵For if we have grown into union with him through a death like his, we shall also be united with him in the resurrection. ⁶We know that our old self was crucified with him, so that our sinful body might be done away with, that we might no longer be in slavery to sin. ⁷For a dead person has been absolved from sin.
Holy Mary...

5. Galatians 3:23-29 Hail Mary...

Jesus in the mystery of Your Baptism. ²³Before faith came, we were held in custody under law, confined for the faith that was to be revealed. ²⁴Consequently, the law was our disciplinarian for Christ, that we might be justified by faith. ²⁵But now that faith has come, we are no longer under a disciplinarian. ²⁶For through faith you are all children of God in Christ Jesus. ²⁷For all of you who were baptized into Christ have clothed your-selves with Christ. ²⁸There is neither Jew nor Greek, there is neither slave nor free person, there is not male and female; for you are all one in Christ Jesus. ²⁹And if you belong to Christ, then you are Abraham's descendant, heirs according to the promise.
Holy Mary...

6. Luke 22:40-46 Hail Mary...

Jesus in the mystery of the Agony in the Garden. ⁴⁰When he arrived at the place he said to them, "Pray that you may not undergo the test." [41]After withdrawing about a stone's throw from them and kneeling, he prayed, [42]saying, "Father, if you are willing, take this cup away from me; still, not my will but yours be done." [43]And to strengthen him an angel from heaven appeared to him. [44]He was in such agony and he prayed so fervently that his sweat became like drops of blood falling on the ground. [45]When he rose from prayer and returned to his disciples, he found them sleeping from grief. [46]He said to them, "Why are you sleeping? Get up and pray that you may not undergo the test."

Holy Mary...

7. Ephesians 1:7-10 Hail Mary...

Jesus in the mystery of the Agony in the Garden. [7]In him we have redemption by his blood, the forgiveness of transgressions, in accord with the riches of his grace [8]that he lavished upon us. In all wisdom and insight, [9]he has made known to us the mystery of his will in accord with his favor that he set forth in him [10]as a plan for the fullness of times, to sum up all things in Christ, in heaven and on earth. **Galatians 1:3-5** [3]Grace to you and peace from God our Father and the Lord Jesus Christ, [4]who gave himself for our sins that he might rescue us from the present evil age in accord with the will of our God and Father, [5]to whom be glory forever and ever. Amen.

Holy Mary...

8. Romans 6:8-14 Hail Mary...

Jesus in the mystery of Your Resurrection. [8]If, then, we have died with Christ, we believe that we shall also live with him. [9]We know that Christ, raised from the dead, dies no more; death no longer has power over him. [10]As to his death, he died to sin once and for all; as to his life, he lives for God. [11]Consequently, you too must think of yourselves as (being) dead to sin and living for God in Christ Jesus. [12]Therefore, sin must not reign over your mortal bodies so that you obey their desires. [13]And do not present the parts of your bodies to sin as weapons for wickedness, but present yourselves to God as raised from the dead to life and the parts of your bodies to God as weapons for righteousness. [14]For sin is not to have any power over you, since you are not under the law but under grace.

Holy Mary...

9. Ephesians 2:1-10 Hail Mary...

Jesus in the mystery of Your Resurrection. [1]You were dead in your transgressions and sins [2]in which you once lived following the age of this world, following the ruler of the power of the air, the spirit that is now at work in the disobedient. [3]All of us once lived among them in the desires of our flesh, following the wishes of the flesh and the impulses, and we were by nature children of wrath, like the rest. [4]But God, who is rich in mercy, because of the great love he had for us, [5]even when we were dead in our transgressions, brought us to life with Christ (by grace you have been saved), [6]raised us up with him, and seated us with him in the heavens in Christ Jesus, [7]that in the ages to come he might show the immeasurable riches of his grace in his kindness to us in Christ Jesus. [8]For by grace you have been saved through faith, and this is not from you; it is the gift of God; [9]it is not from works, so no one may boast. [10]For we are his handiwork, created in Christ Jesus for the good works that God has prepared in advance, that we should live in them.

Holy Mary...

10. Hail Mary...

Deliver us, Lord, we pray, from every evil, graciously grant peace in our days, that, by the help of your mercy, we may be always free from sin and safe from all distress, as we await the blessed hope and the coming of our Savior, Jesus Christ. We ask You for an increase in the gifts of the Holy Spirit: that we may come to know You clearer, follow You nearer, and love You dearer;

Holy Mary...

Glory be...

Oh my Jesus...

THE SECOND SACRED MYSTERIES OF THE ROSARY OF OUR REDEMPTION

The joy of the Visitation was illuminated by Your miracle at the Wedding Feast of Cana. You ransomed us through the sorrow and shedding of Your blood during the Scourging at the Pillar and revealed our redemption in Your Glorious Ascension.

Rosary Reflections

Our Father...

1. James 4:7-8 Hail Mary...

   ⁷So submit yourselves to God. Resist the devil, and he
   will flee from you. ⁸Draw near to God, and he will draw
   near to you. We ask You to send us Your Holy Spirit to
   enlighten us in our understanding of these mysteries of
   our redemption;

   Holy Mary...

2. Colossians 3:12-17 Hail Mary...

   Jesus in the mystery of the Visitation. ¹²Put on then,
   as God's chosen ones, holy and beloved, heartfelt compassion, kindness, humility, gentleness, and patience,
   ¹³bearing with one another and forgiving one another, if
   one has a grievance against another; as the Lord has for-
   given you, so must you also do. ¹⁴And over all these put on
   love, that is, the bond of perfection. ¹⁵And let the peace of
   Christ control your hearts, the peace into which you were
   also called in one body. And be thankful. ¹⁶Let the word
   of Christ dwell in you richly, as in all wisdom you teach
   and admonish one another, singing psalms, hymns, and
   spiritual songs with gratitude in your hearts to God. ¹⁷And
   whatever you do, in word or in deed, do everything in the
   name of the Lord Jesus, giving thanks to God the Father
   through him.

   Holy Mary...

3. 1 John 3:13-16 Hail Mary...

   Jesus in the mystery of the Visitation. ¹³Do not be amazed,
   (then,) brothers, if the world hates you. ¹⁴We know that we
   have passed from death to life because we love our brothers. Whoever does not love remains in death. ¹⁵Everyone
   who hates his brother is a murderer, and you know that no
   murderer has eternal life remaining in him. ¹⁶The way we

came to know love was that he laid down his life for us; so
we ought to lay down our lives for our brothers.
Holy Mary...

4. Genesis 2:22-24 Hail Mary...

Jesus in the mystery of the Wedding Feast at Cana. [22]The
LORD God then built up into a woman the rib that he
had taken from the man. When he brought her to the man,
[23]the man said: "This one, at last, is bone of my bones and
flesh of my flesh; This one shall be called 'woman,' for out
of 'her man' this one has been taken." [24]That is why a man
leaves his father and mother and clings to his wife, and the
two of them become one body.

John 13:34-35 [34]I give you a new commandment: love
one another. As I have loved you, so you also should love
one another. [35]This is how all will know that you are my
disciples, if you have love for one another."
Holy Mary...

5. Ephesians 5:25-33 Hail Mary...

Jesus in the mystery of the Wedding Feast at Cana. [25]Hus-
bands, love your wives, even as Christ loved the church
and handed himself over for her [26]to sanctify her, cleansing her by the bath of water with the word, [27]that he might
present to himself the church in splendor, without spot
or wrinkle or any such thing, that she might be holy and
without blemish. [28]So (also) husbands should love their
wives as their own bodies. He who loves his wife loves
himself. [29]For no one hates his own flesh but rather nour-
ishes and cherishes it, even as Christ does the church,
[30]because we are members of his body. [31]"For this reason
a man shall leave his father and his mother and be joined
to his wife and the two shall become one flesh." [32]This is
a great mystery, but I speak in reference to Christ and the

church. [33]In any case, each one of you should love his wife as himself,
Holy Mary...

6. John 15:1-13 Hail Mary...

Jesus in the mystery of the Scourging at the Pillar. [1]"I am the true vine, and my Father is the vine grower. [2]He takes away every branch in me that does not bear fruit, and every one that does he prunes so that it bears more fruit. [3]You are already pruned because of the word that I spoke to you. [4]Remain in me, as I remain in you. Just as a branch cannot bear fruit on its own unless it remains on the vine, so neither can you unless you remain in me. [5]I am the vine, you are the branches. Whoever remains in me and I in him will bear much fruit, because without me you can do nothing. [6] Anyone who does not remain in me will be thrown out like a branch and wither; people will gather them and throw them into a fire and they will be burned. [7]If you remain in me and my words remain in you, ask for whatever you want and it will be done for you. [8]By this is my Father glorified, that you bear much fruit and become my disciples. [9]As the Father loves me, so I also love you. Remain in my love. [10]If you keep my commandments, you will remain in my love, just as I have kept my Father's commandments and remain in his love. [11]"I have told you this so that my joy may be in you and your joy may be complete. [12]This is my commandment: love one another as I love you. [13]No one has greater love than this, to lay down one's life for one's friends.
Holy Mary...

7. John 16:20-28 Hail Mary...

Jesus in the mystery of the Scourging at the Pillar. [20]Amen, amen, I say to you, you will weep and mourn, while the world rejoices; you will grieve, but your grief will become

joy. [21]When a woman is in labor, she is in anguish because her hour has arrived; but when she has given birth to a child, she no longer remembers the pain because of her joy that a child has been born into the world. [22]So you also are now in anguish. But I will see you again, and your hearts will rejoice, and no one will take your joy away from you. [23]On that day you will not question me about anything. Amen, amen, I say to you, whatever you ask the Father in my name he will give you. [24]Until now you have not asked anything in my name; ask and you will receive, so that your joy may be complete. [25]"I have told you this in figures of speech. The hour is coming when I will no longer speak to you in figures but I will tell you clearly about the Father. [26]On that day you will ask in my name, and I do not tell you that I will ask the Father for you. [27]For the Father himself loves you, because you have loved me and have come to believe that I came from God. [28]I came from the Father and have come into the world.
Holy Mary...

8. Colossians 3:1-10 Hail Mary...

Jesus in the mystery of Your Ascension. [1]If then you were raised with Christ, seek what is above, where Christ is seated at the right hand of God. [2]Think of what is above, not of what is on earth. [3]For you have died, and your life is hidden with Christ in God. [4]When Christ your life appears, then you too will appear with him in glory. [5]Put to death, then, the parts of you that are earthly: immorality, impurity, passion, evil desire, and the greed that is idolatry. [6]Because of these the wrath of God is coming (upon the disobedient). [7]By these you too once conducted yourselves, when you lived in that way. [8]But now you must put them all away: anger, fury, malice, slander, and obscene language out of your mouths. [9]Stop lying to one another, since you have taken off the old self with its

practices [10]and have put on the new self, which is being renewed, for knowledge, in the image of its creator.
Holy Mary...

9. John 14:1-3 Hail Mary...

Jesus in the mystery of Your Ascension. [1]"Do not let your hearts be troubled. You have faith in God; have faith also in me. [2]In my Father's house there are many dwelling places. If there were not, would I have told you that I am going to prepare a place for you? [3]And if I go and prepare a place for you, I will come back again and take you to myself, so that where I am you also may be.
Holy Mary...

10. Hail Mary...

Deliver us, Lord, we pray, from every evil, graciously grant peace in our days, that, by the help of your mercy, we may be always free from sin and safe from all distress, as we await the blessed hope and the coming of our Savior, Jesus Christ. We ask You for an increase in the gifts of the Holy Spirit: that we may come to know You clearer, follow You nearer, and love You dearer;
Holy Mary...

Glory be...

Oh my Jesus...

The Third Sacred Mysteries of the Rosary of our Redemption

The joy of the Nativity was illuminated by Your proclamation of the Gospels. You ransomed us through the sorrow and shedding of Your blood during the Crowning with Thorns and revealed our redemption in the Glorious Descent of the Holy Spirit.

Our Father...

1. James 4:7-8 Hail Mary...
   ⁷So submit yourselves to God. Resist the devil, and he
   will flee from you. ⁸Draw near to God, and he will draw
   near to you. We ask You to send us Your Holy Spirit to
   enlighten us in our understanding of these mysteries of
   our redemption;
   Holy Mary...

2. Colossians 1:15-18 Hail Mary...
   Jesus in the mystery of the Nativity. ¹⁵He is the image of
   the invisible God, the firstborn of all creation. ¹⁶For in
   him were created all things in heaven and on earth, the
   visible and the invisible, whether thrones or dominions or
   principalities or powers; all things were created through
   him and for him. ¹⁷He is before all things, and in him
   all things hold together. ¹⁸He is the head of the body, the
   church. He is the beginning, the firstborn from the dead,
   that in all things he himself might be preeminent.
   Holy Mary...

3. 2 Corinthians 6:16-18 Hail Mary...
   Jesus in the mystery of the Nativity. ¹⁶For we are the
   temple of the living God; as God said: "I will live with
   them and move among them, and I will be their God and
   they shall be my people. ¹⁷Therefore, come forth from
   them and be separate," says the Lord, "and touch nothing
   unclean; then I will receive you ¹⁸and I will be a father to
   you, and you shall be sons and daughters to me, says the
   Lord Almighty."
   Holy Mary...

4. 2 Corinthians 4:1-6 Hail Mary...
   Jesus in the mystery of Your proclamation of the Gospels.
   ¹Therefore, since we have this ministry through the mercy
   shown us, we are not discouraged. ²Rather, we have

renounced shameful, hidden things; not acting deceitfully or falsifying the word of God, but by the open declaration of the truth we commend ourselves to everyone's conscience in the sight of God. ³And even though our gospel is veiled, it is veiled for those who are perishing, ⁴in whose case the god of this age has blinded the minds of the unbelievers, so that they may not see the light of the gospel of the glory of Christ, who is the image of God. ⁵For we do not preach ourselves but Jesus Christ as Lord, and ourselves as your slaves for the sake of Jesus. ⁶For God who said, "Let light shine out of darkness," has shone in our hearts to bring to light the knowledge of the glory of God on the face of Jesus Christ.
Holy Mary...

5. 1 Corinthians 1:17-18 Hail Mary...

Jesus in the mystery of Your proclamation of the Gospels. ¹⁷For Christ did not send me to baptize but to preach the gospel, and not with the wisdom of human eloquence, so that the cross of Christ might not be emptied of its meaning. ¹⁸The message of the cross is foolishness to those who are perishing, but to us who are being saved it is the power of God.
Holy Mary...

6. Galatians 6:7-10 Hail Mary...

Jesus in the mystery of the Crowning with Thorns. ⁷Make no mistake: God is not mocked, for a person will reap only what he sows, ⁸because the one who sows for his flesh will reap corruption from the flesh, but the one who sows for the spirit will reap eternal life from the spirit. ⁹Let us not grow tired of doing good, for in due time we shall reap our harvest, if we do not give up. ¹⁰So then, while we have the opportunity, let us do good to all, but especially to those who belong to the family of the faith.
Holy Mary...

7. Ephesians 3:14-21 Hail Mary...

Jesus in the mystery of the Crowning with Thorns. [14]For this reason I kneel before the Father, [15]from whom every family in heaven and on earth is named, [16]that he may grant you in accord with the riches of his glory to be strengthened with power through his Spirit in the inner self, [17]and that Christ may dwell in your hearts through faith; that you, rooted and grounded in love, [18]may have strength to comprehend with all the holy ones what is the breadth and length and height and depth, [19]and to know the love of Christ that surpasses knowledge, so that you may be filled with all the fullness of God. [20]Now to him who is able to accomplish far more than all we ask or imagine, by the power at work within us, [21]to him be glory in the church and in Christ Jesus to all generations, forever and ever. Amen.

Holy Mary...

8. Romans 8:1-4 Hail Mary...

Jesus in the mystery of the Descent of the Holy Spirit. [1]Hence, now there is no condemnation for those who are in Christ Jesus. [2]For the law of the spirit of life in Christ Jesus has freed you from the law of sin and death. [3]For what the law, weakened by the flesh, was powerless to do, this God has done: by sending his own Son in the likeness of sinful flesh and for the sake of sin, he condemned sin in the flesh, [4]so that the righteous decree of the law might be fulfilled in us, who live not according to the flesh but according to the spirit.

Holy Mary...

9. Galatians 5:16-25 Hail Mary...

Jesus in the mystery of the Descent of the Holy Spirit. [16]I say, then: live by the Spirit and you will certainly not gratify the desire of the flesh. [17]For the flesh has desires against the Spirit, and the Spirit against the flesh; these are opposed to each other, so that you may not do what you want. [18]But if you are guided by the Spirit, you are not under the law. [19]Now the works of the flesh are obvious: immorality, impurity, licentiousness, [20]idolatry, sorcery, hatreds, rivalry, jealousy, outbursts of fury, acts of selfishness, dissensions, factions, [21]occasions of envy, drinking bouts, orgies, and the like. I warn you, as I warned you before, that those who do such things will not inherit the kingdom of God. [22]In contrast, the fruit of the Spirit is love, joy, peace, patience, kindness, generosity, faithfulness, [23]gentleness, self-control. Against such there is no law. [24]Now those who belong to Christ (Jesus) have crucified their flesh with its passions and desires. [25]If we live in the Spirit, let us also follow the Spirit.

Holy Mary...

10. Hail Mary...

Deliver us, Lord, we pray, from every evil, graciously grant peace in our days, that, by the help of your mercy, we may be always free from sin and safe from all distress, as we await the blessed hope and the coming of our Savior, Jesus Christ. We ask You for an increase in the gifts of the Holy Spirit: that we may come to know You clearer, follow You nearer, and love You dearer;

Holy Mary...

Glory be...

Oh my Jesus...

THE FOURTH SACRED MYSTERIES OF THE ROSARY OF OUR REDEMPTION

The joy of the Presentation was illuminated by Your Transfiguration. You ransomed us through the sorrow and shedding of Your blood during the Carrying of the Cross and revealed our redemption in the Glorious Assumption of Your Blessed Mother into heaven.

Our Father...

1. James 4:7-8 Hail Mary...

⁷So submit yourselves to God. Resist the devil, and he will flee from you. ⁸Draw near to God, and he will draw near to you. We ask You to send us Your Holy Spirit to enlighten us in our understanding of these mysteries of our redemption; **Holy Mary...**

2. 2 Corinthians 6:1-2 Hail Mary...

Jesus in the mystery of the Presentation. ¹Working together, then, we appeal to you not to receive the grace of God in vain. ²For he says: "In an acceptable time I heard you, and on the day of salvation I helped you." Behold, now is a very acceptable time; behold, now is the day of salvation. **Holy Mary...**

3. Jude 1:17-25 Hail Mary...

Jesus in the mystery of the Presentation. ¹⁷But you, beloved, remember the words spoken beforehand by the apostles of our Lord Jesus Christ, ¹⁸for they told you, "In (the) last time there will be scoffers who will live according to their own godless desires." ¹⁹These are the ones who cause divisions; they live on the natural plane, devoid of the Spirit. ²⁰But you, beloved, build yourselves up in your most holy faith; pray in the Holy Spirit. ²¹Keep your selves in the love of God and wait for the mercy of our Lord Jesus Christ that leads to eternal life. ²²On those who waver, have mercy; ²³save others by snatching them out of the fire; on others have mercy with fear, abhorring even the outer garment stained by the flesh. ²⁴To the one who is able to keep you from stumbling and to present you unblemished and exultant, in the presence of his glory, ²⁵to the only God, our savior, through Jesus Christ our Lord be glory, majesty, power, and authority from ages past, now, and for ages to come. Amen. **Holy Mary..**

4. 1 Peter 1:3-9 Hail Mary...

Jesus in the mystery of your Transfiguration. ³Blessed be the God and Father of our Lord Jesus Christ, who in his great mercy gave us a new birth to a living hope through the resurrection of Jesus Christ from the dead, ⁴to an inheritance that is imperishable, undefiled, and unfading, kept in heaven for you ⁵who by the power of God are safeguarded through faith, to a salvation that is ready to be revealed in the final time. ⁶In this you rejoice, although now for a little while you may have to suffer through various trials, ⁷so that the genuineness of your faith, more precious than gold that is perishable even though tested by fire, may prove to be for praise, glory, and honor at the revelation of Jesus Christ. ⁸Although you have not seen him you love him; even though you do not see him now yet believe in him, you rejoice with an indescribable and glorious joy, ⁹as you attain the goal of (your) faith, the salvation of your souls.

Holy Mary...

5. 2 Corinthians 3:11, 17-18 Hail Mary...

Jesus in the mystery of Your Transfiguration. ¹¹For if what was going to fade was glorious, how much more will what endures be glorious. ¹⁷Now the Lord is the Spirit, and where the Spirit of the Lord is, there is freedom. ¹⁸All of us, gazing with unveiled face on the glory of the Lord, are being transformed into the same image from glory to glory, as from the Lord who is the Spirit.

Holy Mary...

6. Hebrews 12:1-4, 12-14 Hail Mary...

Jesus in the mystery of the Carrying of the Cross. ¹Therefore, since we are surrounded by so great a cloud of witnesses, let us rid ourselves of every burden and sin that clings to us and persevere in running the race that lies before us ²while keeping our eyes fixed on Jesus, the

leader and perfecter of faith. For the sake of the joy that lay before him he endured the cross, despising its shame, and has taken his seat at the right of the throne of God. [3]Consider how he endured such opposition from sinners, in order that you may not grow weary and lose heart. [4]In your struggle against sin you have not yet resisted to the point of shedding blood. [12]So strengthen your drooping hands and your weak knees. [13]Make straight paths for your feet, that what is lame may not be dislocated but healed. [14]Strive for peace with everyone, and for that holiness without which no one will see the Lord.
Holy Mary...

7. 2 Corinthians 2:14-16 Hail Mary...

Jesus in the mystery of the Carrying of the Cross. [14]But thanks be to God, who always leads us in triumph in Christ and manifests through us the odor of the knowledge of him in every place. [15]For we are the aroma of Christ for God among those who are being saved and among those who are perishing, [16]to the latter an odor of death that leads to death, to the former an odor of life that leads to life.
Holy Mary...

8. Genesis 3:15 Hail Mary...

Jesus in the mystery of the Assumption of Your Blessed Mother into heaven. [15]I will put enmity between you and the woman, and between your offspring and hers; He will strike at your head, while you strike at his heel."
Holy Mary...

9. Isaiah 55:10-11 Hail Mary...

Jesus in the mystery of the Assumption of Your Blessed Mother into heaven. [10]For just as from the heavens the rain and snow come down And do not return there till they have watered the earth, making it fertile and fruitful,

Giving seed to him who sows and bread to him who eats, [11]So shall my word be that goes forth from my mouth; It shall not return to me void, but shall do my will, achieving the end for which I sent it.

Holy Mary...

10. Hail Mary...

Deliver us, Lord, we pray, from every evil, graciously grant peace in our days, that, by the help of your mercy, we may be always free from sin and safe from all distress, as we await the blessed hope and the coming of our Savior, Jesus Christ. We ask You for an increase in the gifts of the Holy Spirit: that we may come to know You clearer, follow You nearer, and love You dearer;

Holy Mary...

Glory be...

Oh my Jesus...

The Fifth
Sacred Mysteries
of the Rosary of our
Redemption

The joy of Finding the Child Jesus in the Temple was illuminated by Your Institution of the Eucharist. You ransomed us through the sorrow and shedding of Your blood in the Crucifixion and revealed our redemption in the Glorious Coronation of Your Blessed Mother as Queen of Heaven and Earth.

Our Father...

1. James 4:7-8 Hail Mary...

⁷So submit yourselves to God. Resist the devil, and he will flee from you. ⁸Draw near to God, and he will draw near to you. We ask You to send us Your Holy Spirit to enlighten us in our understanding of these mysteries of our redemption;

Holy Mary...

2. Isaiah 55:6-9 Hail Mary...

Jesus in the mystery of Finding the Child Jesus in the Temple. ⁶Seek the LORD while he may be found, call him while he is near. ⁷Let the scoundrel forsake his way, and the wicked man his thoughts; Let him turn to the LORD for mercy; to our God, who is generous in forgiving. ⁸For my thoughts are not your thoughts, nor are your ways my ways, says the LORD. ⁹As high as the heavens are above the earth, so high are my ways above your ways and my thoughts above your thoughts.

Matthew 5:9 ⁹Blessed are the peacemakers, for they will be called children of God.

Holy Mary...

3. 1 Peter 2:9-10 Hail Mary...

Jesus in the mystery of Finding the Child Jesus in the Temple. ⁹But you are "a chosen race, a royal priesthood, a holy nation, a people of his own, so that you may announce the praises" of him who called you out of darkness into his wonderful light. ¹⁰Once you were "no people" but now you are God's people; you "had not received mercy" but now you have received mercy.

Matthew 5:7 ⁷Blessed are the merciful, for they will be shown mercy.

Holy Mary...

4. John 6:26-29 Hail Mary...

Jesus in the mystery of Your Institution of the Eucharist. [26]Jesus answered them and said, "Amen, amen, I say to you, you are looking for me not because you saw signs but because you ate the loaves and were filled. [27]Do not work for food that perishes but for the food that endures for eternal life, which the Son of Man will give you. For on him the Father, God, has set his seal." [28]So they said to him, "What can we do to accomplish the works of God?" [29]Jesus answered and said to them, "This is the work of God, that you believe in the one he sent."

Matthew 5:6 [6]Blessed are they who hunger and thirst for righteousness, they will be satisfied.

Holy Mary...

5. Ephesians 6:10-17 Hail Mary...

Jesus in the mystery of Your Institution of the Eucharist. [10]Finally, draw your strength from the Lord and from his mighty power. [11]Put on the armor of God so that you may be able to stand firm against the tactics of the devil. [12]For our struggle is not with flesh and blood but with the principalities, with the powers, with the world rulers of this present darkness, with the evil spirits in the heavens. [13]Therefore, put on the armor of God, that you may be able to resist on the evil day and, having done everything, to hold your ground. [14]So stand fast with your loins girded in truth, clothed with righteousness as a breastplate, [15]and your feet shod in readiness for the gospel of peace. [16]In all circumstances, hold faith as a shield, to quench all (the) flaming arrows of the evil one. [17]And take the helmet of salvation and the sword of the Spirit, which is the word of God.

Matthew 5:11-12 [11]Blessed are you when they insult you and persecute you and utter every kind of evil against you falsely because of me. [12]Rejoice and be glad, for your reward will be great in heaven. Thus they persecuted the prophets who were before you.

Holy Mary...

6. Isaiah 53:1-12 Hail Mary...

Jesus in the mystery of the Crucifixion. [1]Who would believe what we have heard? To whom has the arm of the LORD been revealed? [2]He grew up like a sapling before him, like a shoot from the parched earth; There was in him no stately bearing to make us look at him, nor appearance that would attract us to him. [3]He was spurned and avoided by men, a man of suffering, accustomed to infirmity, One of those from whom men hide their faces, spurned, and we held him in no esteem. [4]Yet it was our infirmities that he bore, our sufferings that he endured, While we thought of him as stricken, as one smitten by God and afflicted. [5]But he was pierced for our offenses, crushed for our sins, Upon him was the chastisement that makes us whole, by his stripes we were healed. [6]We had all gone astray like sheep, each following his own way; But the LORD laid upon him the guilt of us all. [7]Though he was harshly treated, he submitted and opened not his mouth; Like a lamb led to the slaughter or a sheep before the shearers, he was silent and opened not his mouth. [8]Oppressed and condemned, he was taken away, and who would have thought any more of his destiny? When he was cut off from the land of the living, and smitten for the sin of his people, [9]A grave was assigned him among the wicked and a burial place with evildoers, Though he had done no wrong nor spoken any falsehood. [10](But the LORD was pleased to crush him in infirmity.) If he gives his life as an offering for sin, he shall see his descendants in a long life, and the will of the LORD shall be accomplished through him. [11]Because of his affliction he shall see the light in fullness of days; Through his suffering, my servant shall justify many, and their guilt he shall bear.

¹²Therefore I will give him his portion among the great, and he shall divide the spoils with the mighty, Because he surrendered himself to death and was counted among the wicked; And he shall take away the sins of many, and win pardon for their offenses.

Matthew 5:5 ⁵Blessed are the meek, for they will inherit the land.

Holy Mary...

7. Luke 23:34 Hail Mary...

Jesus in the mystery of the Crucifixion. ³⁴Then Jesus said, "Father, forgive them, they know not what they do."

Galatians 2:19-20 ¹⁹For through the law I died to the law, that I might live for God. I have been crucified with Christ; ²⁰yet I live, no longer I, but Christ lives in me; insofar as I now live in the flesh, I live by faith in the Son of God who has loved me and given himself up for me.

Luke 23:43 "Amen, I say to you, today you will be with me in Paradise."

Matthew 5:4, 5:10 ⁴Blessed are they who mourn, for they will be comforted. ¹⁰Blessed are they who are persecuted for the sake of righteousness, for theirs is the kingdom of heaven.

Holy Mary...

8. Revelation 11:15-19 Hail Mary...

Jesus in the mystery of the Coronation of Your Blessed Mother as Queen of Heaven and Earth. ¹⁵Then the seventh angel blew his trumpet. There were loud voices in heaven, saying, "The kingdom of the world now belongs to our Lord and to his Anointed, and he will reign forever and ever." ¹⁶The twenty-four elders who sat on their thrones before God prostrated themselves and worshiped God ¹⁷and said: "We give thanks to you, Lord God almighty, who is and who were. For you have assumed your great power and have established your reign. ¹⁸The nations

raged, but your wrath has come, and the time for the dead to be judged, and to recompense your servants, the prophets, and the holy ones and those who fear your name, the small and the great alike, and to destroy those who destroy the earth." [19]Then God's temple in heaven was opened, and the ark of his covenant could be seen in the temple. **Matthew 5:3** [3]"Blessed are the poor in spirit, for theirs is the kingdom of heaven.
Holy Mary...

9. 2 John 1:1-3 Hail Mary...

Jesus in the mystery of the Coronation of Your Blessed Mother as Queen of Heaven and Earth. [1]The Presbyter to the chosen Lady and to her children whom I love in truth—and not only I but also all who know the truth— [2]because of the truth that dwells in us and will be with us forever. [3]Grace, mercy, and peace will be with us from God the Father and from Jesus Christ the Father's Son in truth and love.
Matthew 5:8 [8]Blessed are the pure of heart, for they will see God.
Holy Mary...

10. Hail Mary...

Deliver us, Lord, we pray, from every evil, graciously grant peace in our days, that, by the help of your mercy, we may be always free from sin and safe from all distress, as we await the blessed hope and the coming of our Savior, Jesus Christ. We ask You for an increase in the gifts of the Holy Spirit: that we may come to know You clearer, follow You nearer, and love You dearer;
Holy Mary...

Glory be...

Oh my Jesus...

Hail, Holy Queen... (pg. 5)

Let us pray. Oh God, whose only begotten Son...
(pg. 4)

St. Michael the Archangel... (pg. 5)

Psalm 23:1-6 [1]A psalm of David. The LORD is my shepherd; there is nothing I lack. [2]In green pastures you let me graze; to safe waters you lead me; [3]you restore my strength. You guide me along the right path for the sake of your name. [4]Even when I walk through a dark valley, I fear no harm for you are at my side; your rod and staff give me courage. [5] You set a table before me as my enemies watch; You anoint my head with oil; my cup overflows. [6]Only goodness and love will pursue me all the days of my life; I will dwell in the house of the LORD for years to come.

For the intentions of the Holy Father:

   Our Father...

   Hail Mary...

   Glory be...

In the beginning was the Word... (pg. 209)

THE TIMELESS MEDITATION ON THE MASS ROSARY

The Timeless Meditation on the Mass Rosary blends the traditional prayers of the Rosary, viewed in a timeless way, with a prayerful study of the upcoming Order of Mass. After praying this Rosary in advance of an upcoming Liturgy, we will come to Mass better prepared to receive both the Word of God and the Holy Eucharist. Yes, His words will burn in our hearts as He opens up the Scripture verses to us and our eyes will be opened to recognize Him in the breaking of the bread.

This Rosary can be prayed when making a Holy Hour during the time before attending Holy Mass. You will get so much more out of participation in the liturgies of the Word and the Eucharist by getting prepared through this Rosary prayer.

Rosary Reflections

1. **Lovely Lady dressed in blue...** (pg. 1)

2. **Come, Holy Spirit...** (pg. 2)

3. **Hail bright star of ocean...** (pg. 3)

4. **Let us pray. Oh God, whose only begotten Son...** (pg. 4)

5. (Sign of the Cross)
   In the name of the Father...

I Believe in God... (Apostles' Creed, pg. 4)

Our Father...

Hail Mary...
Jesus, we ask You for an increase in the gift of Faith:
(Hebrews 11:1-3, 6, pg. 6)
Holy Mary...

Hail Mary...
Jesus, we ask You for an increase in the gift of Hope:
(Romans 8:14-28, pg. 6)
Holy Mary...

Hail Mary...
Jesus, we ask You for an increase in the gift of Love:
(1 Corinthians 13:1-13, pg. 7)
Holy Mary...

Glory be...

Oh my Jesus... (Fatima Prayer, pg. 5)

THE FIRST
SACRED MYSTERIES
OF THE ROSARY OF OUR
REDEMPTION

The joy of the Annunciation was illuminated by Your Baptism. You ransomed us through the sorrow and shedding of Your blood during the Agony in the Garden and revealed our redemption in Your Glorious Resurrection.

Our Father...

1. Hail Mary...
Jesus, we ask You to send us Your Holy Spirit to enlighten us in our understanding of these mysteries of our redemption;
Holy Mary...

2. Hail Mary...
Jesus in the mystery of the Annunciation.
Entrance Antiphon: ...
Holy Mary...

3. Hail Mary...
Jesus in the mystery of the Annunciation. May the grace of our Lord Jesus Christ and the love of God and the fellowship of the Holy Spirit be with you all. **(And with your spirit.)**
Holy Mary...

4. Hail Mary...
Jesus in the mystery of Your Baptism. Grace to you and peace from God our Father and the Lord Jesus Christ. **(And with your spirit.)**
Holy Mary...

5. Hail Mary...
Jesus in the mystery of Your Baptism. The Lord be with you. **(And with your spirit.)**
Holy Mary...

6. Hail Mary...
Jesus in the mystery of the Agony in the Garden. I confess to Almighty God and to you my brothers and sisters, that I have sinned, in my thoughts and in my words, in what I have done and in what I have failed to do, (and striking their breast, they say) through my fault, through my fault, through my most grievous fault; therefore I ask Blessed

Mary ever Virgin, all the Angels and Saints, and you, my brothers and sisters to pray for me to the Lord our God.
Holy Mary...

7. **Hail Mary...**
Jesus in the mystery of the Agony in the Garden. Have mercy on us, O Lord. For we have sinned against You; Show us, O Lord your mercy. And grant us your salvation.
Holy Mary...

8. **Hail Mary...**
Jesus in the mystery of Your Resurrection. Glory to God in the highest, and on earth peace to people of good will. We praise you, we bless you, we adore you, we glorify you, we give you thanks for your great glory, Lord God, heavenly King, O God almighty Father. Lord Jesus Christ, Only Begotten Son, Lord God, Lamb of God, Son of the Father, you take away the sin of the world, have mercy on us; you take away the sin of the world receive our prayer; you are seated at the right hand of the Father, have mercy on us.
Holy Mary...

9. **Hail Mary...**
Jesus in the mystery of Your Resurrection. For you alone are the Holy One, you alone are the Lord, you alone are the Most High, Jesus Christ, with the Holy Spirit, in the glory of God the Father. Amen.
Holy Mary...

10. **Hail Mary...**
Jesus, we ask You for an increase in the gifts of the Holy Spirit: that we may come to know You clearer, follow You nearer, and love You dearer;
Holy Mary...

Glory be...

Oh my Jesus...

The Second Sacred Mysteries of the Rosary of our Redemption

The joy of the Visitation was illuminated by Your miracle at the Wedding Feast of Cana. You ransomed us through the sorrow and shedding of Your blood during the Scourging at the Pillar and revealed our redemption in Your Glorious Ascension.

Our Father...

1. Hail Mary...
Jesus, we ask You to send us Your Holy Spirit to enlighten us in our understanding of these mysteries of our redemption;
Holy Mary...

2. Hail Mary...
Jesus in the mystery of the Visitation.
Entrance Antiphon: ...
Holy Mary...

3. Hail Mary...
Jesus in the mystery of the Visitation. May the grace of our Lord Jesus Christ and the love of God and the fellowship of the Holy Spirit be with you all. **(And with your spirit.)**
Holy Mary...

4. Hail Mary...
Jesus in the mystery of the Wedding Feast at Cana. Grace to you and peace from God our Father and the Lord Jesus Christ. **(And with your spirit.)**
Holy Mary...

5. Hail Mary...
Jesus in the mystery of the Wedding Feast at Cana. The Lord be with you. **(And with your spirit.)**
Holy Mary...

6. Hail Mary...
Jesus in the mystery of the Scourging at the Pillar. I confess to Almighty God and to you my brothers and sisters, that I have sinned, in my thoughts and in my words, in what I have done and in what I have failed to do, (and striking their breast, they say) through my fault, through my fault, through my most grievous fault; therefore I ask Blessed

Mary ever Virgin, all the Angels and Saints, and you, my brothers and sisters to pray for me to the Lord our God.
Holy Mary...

7. Hail Mary...

Jesus in the mystery of the Scourging at the Pillar. Have mercy on us, O Lord. For we have sinned against You; Show us, O Lord your mercy. And grant us your salvation.
Holy Mary...

8. Hail Mary...

Jesus in the mystery of Your Ascension. Glory to God in the highest, and on earth peace to people of good will. We praise you, we bless you, we adore you, we glorify you, we give you thanks for your great glory, Lord God, heavenly King, O God almighty Father. Lord Jesus Christ, Only Begotten Son, Lord God, Lamb of God, Son of the Father, you take away the sin of the world, have mercy on us; you take away the sin of the world receive our prayer; you are seated at the right hand of the Father, have mercy on us.
Holy Mary...

9. Hail Mary...

Jesus in the mystery of Your Resurrection. For you alone are the Holy One, you alone are the Lord, you alone are the Most High, Jesus Christ, with the Holy Spirit, in the glory of God the Father. Amen.
Holy Mary...

10. Hail Mary...

Jesus, we ask You for an increase in the gifts of the Holy Spirit: that we may come to know You clearer, follow You nearer, and love You dearer;
Holy Mary...

Glory be...

Oh my Jesus...

THE THIRD
SACRED MYSTERIES
OF THE ROSARY OF OUR
REDEMPTION

The joy of the Nativity was illuminated by Your proclamation of the Gospels. You ransomed us through the sorrow and shedding of Your blood during the Crowning with Thorns and revealed our redemption in the Glorious Descent of the Holy Spirit.

Our Father...

1. Hail Mary...

Jesus, we ask You to send us Your Holy Spirit to enlighten us in our understanding of these mysteries of our redemption;

Holy Mary...

2. Hail Mary...

Jesus in the mystery of the Nativity.

The first reading: ...

Holy Mary...

3. Hail Mary...

Jesus in the mystery of the Nativity.

The Psalm Reading: ...

Holy Mary...

4. Hail Mary...

Jesus in the mystery of Your proclamation of the Gospels.

The second reading and Alleluia: ...

Holy Mary...

5. Hail Mary...

Jesus in the mystery of Your proclamation of the Gospels.

The Gospel reading: ...

Holy Mary...

6. Hail Mary...

Jesus in the mystery of the Crowning with Thorns. Holy, Holy, Holy, Lord, God of hosts. Heaven and earth are full of your glory. Hosanna in the highest. Blessed is he who comes in the name of the Lord. Hosanna in the highest.

Holy Mary...

7. Hail Mary...

Jesus in the mystery of the Crowning with Thorns. We proclaim your Death, O Lord, and profess your Resurrection until you come again.

Holy Mary...

8. Hail Mary...

Jesus in the mystery of the Descent of the Holy Spirit. Behold the Lamb of God, behold Him who takes away the sins of the world. Blessed are those called to the supper of the Lamb. Lord I am not worthy that you should enter under my roof, but only say the word and my soul shall be healed.

Holy Mary...

9. Hail Mary...

Jesus in the mystery of the Descent of the Holy Spirit. Communion Song: ...

Holy Mary...

10. Hail Mary...

Jesus, we ask You for an increase in the gifts of the Holy Spirit: that we may come to know You clearer, follow You nearer, and love You dearer;

Holy Mary...

Glory be...

Oh my Jesus...

The Fourth Sacred Mysteries of the Rosary of our Redemption

The joy of the Presentation was illuminated by Your Transfiguration. You ransomed us through the sorrow and shedding of Your blood during the Carrying of the Cross and revealed our redemption in the Glorious Assumption of Your Blessed Mother into heaven.

Our Father...

1. Hail Mary...

Jesus, we ask You to send us Your Holy Spirit to enlighten us in our understanding of these mysteries of our redemption;

Holy Mary...

2. Hail Mary...

Jesus in the mystery of the Presentation.
The first reading: ...

Holy Mary...

3. Hail Mary...

Jesus in the mystery of the Presentation.
The Psalm Reading: ...

Holy Mary...

4. Hail Mary...

Jesus in the mystery of Your Transfiguration.
The second reading and Alleluia: ...

Holy Mary...

5. Hail Mary...

Jesus in the mystery of Your Transfiguration.
The Gospel reading: ...

Holy Mary...

6. Hail Mary...

Jesus in the mystery of the Carrying of the Cross. Holy, Holy, Holy, Lord, God of hosts. Heaven and earth are full of your glory. Hosanna in the highest. Blessed is he who comes in the name of the Lord. Hosanna in the highest.

Holy Mary...

7. Hail Mary...

Jesus in the mystery of the Carrying of the Cross. When we eat this bread and drink this cup, we proclaim your Death, O Lord, until you come again.

Holy Mary...

8. Hail Mary...

Jesus in the mystery of the Assumption of Your Blessed Mother into heaven. Behold the Lamb of God, behold him who takes away the sins of the world. Blessed are those called to the supper of the Lamb. Lord I am not worthy that you should enter under my roof, but only say the word and my soul shall be healed.

Holy Mary...

9. Hail Mary...

Jesus in the mystery of the Assumption of Your Blessed Mother into heaven.

Communion Song: ...

Holy Mary...

10. Hail Mary...

Jesus, we ask You for an increase in the gifts of the Holy Spirit: that we may come to know You clearer, follow You nearer, and love You dearer;

Holy Mary...

Glory be...

Oh my Jesus...

THE FIFTH
SACRED MYSTERIES
OF THE ROSARY OF OUR
REDEMPTION

The joy of Finding the Child Jesus in the Temple was illuminated by Your Institution of the Eucharist. You ransomed us through the sorrow and shedding of Your blood in the Crucifixion and revealed our redemption in the Glorious Coronation of Your Blessed Mother as Queen of Heaven and Earth.

Our Father...

1. Hail Mary...

Jesus, we ask You to send us Your Holy Spirit to enlighten us in our understanding of these mysteries of our redemption; **Holy Mary...**

2. Hail Mary...

Jesus in the mystery of Finding the Child Jesus in the Temple. I believe in one God, the Father almighty, maker of heaven and earth, of all things visible and invisible. **Holy Mary...**

3. Hail Mary...

Jesus in the mystery of Finding the Child Jesus in the Temple. I believe in one Lord Jesus Christ, the Only Begotten Son of God, born of the Father before all ages. God from God, Light from Light, true God from true God, begotten, not made, consubstantial with the Father; Through him all things were made. For us men and for our salvation he came down from heaven, and by the Holy Spirit was incarnate of the Virgin Mary, and became man. For our sake he was crucified under Pontius Pilate, he suffered death and was buried, and rose again on the third day in accordance with the Scriptures. He ascended into heaven and is seated at the right hand of the Father. He will come again in glory to judge the living and the dead and his kingdom will have no end. **Holy Mary...**

4. Hail Mary...

Jesus in the mystery of Your Institution of the Eucharist. I believe in the Holy Spirit, the Lord, the giver of life, who proceeds from the Father and the Son, who with the Father and the Son is adored and glorified, who has spoken through the prophets. **Holy Mary...**

5. Hail Mary...

Jesus in the mystery of Your Institution of the Eucharist. I believe in one, holy, catholic, and apostolic Church. I confess one baptism for the forgiveness of sins and I look forward to the resurrection of the dead and the life of the world to come. Amen.
Holy Mary...

6. Hail Mary...

Jesus in the mystery of the Crucifixion. Holy, Holy, Holy, Lord, God of hosts. Heaven and earth are full of your glory. Hosanna in the highest. Blessed is he who comes in the name of the Lord. Hosanna in the highest.
Holy Mary...

7. Hail Mary...

Jesus in the mystery of the Crucifixion. Save us, savior of the world, for by your Cross and Resurrection you have set us free.
Holy Mary...

8. Hail Mary...

Jesus in the mystery of the Coronation of Your Blessed Mother as Queen of Heaven and Earth. Behold the Lamb of God, behold Him who takes away the sins of the world. Blessed are those called to the supper of the Lamb. Lord I am not worthy that you should enter under my roof, but only say the word and my soul shall be healed.
Holy Mary...

9. Hail Mary...

Jesus in the mystery of the Coronation of Your Blessed Mother as Queen of Heaven and Earth. It was not you who chose me, says the Lord, but I who chose you and appointed you to go and bear fruit, fruit that will last.
Holy Mary...

10. Hail Mary...
Jesus, we ask You for an increase in the gifts of the Holy Spirit: that we may come to know You clearer, follow You nearer, and love You dearer;
Holy Mary...

Glory be...

Oh my Jesus...

Hail, Holy Queen... (pg. 5)

Let us pray. Oh God, whose only begotten Son... (pg. 4)

St. Michael the Archangel... (pg. 5)

For the intentions of the Holy Father:

   Our Father...

   Hail Mary...

   Glory be...

In the beginning was the Word... (pg. 209)

PRAYERS FOR MEDITATION

John 1:1-18

[1]In the beginning was the Word, and the Word was with God, and the Word was God. [2]He was in the beginning with God. [3]All things came to be through him, and without him nothing came to be. What came to be [4]through him was life, and this life was the light of the human race; [5]the light shines in the darkness and the darkness has not overcome it. [6]A man named John was sent from God. [7]He came for testimony, to testify to the light, so that all might believe through him. [8]He was not the light, but came to testify to the light. [9]The true light, which enlightens everyone, was coming into the world. [10]He was in the world, and the world came to be through him, but the world did not know him. [11]He came to what was his own, but his own people did not accept him. [12]But to those who did accept him he gave power to become children of God, to those who believe in his name, [13]who were born not by natural generation nor by human choice nor by a man's decision but of God. [14]And the Word became flesh and made his dwelling among us, and we saw his glory, the glory as of the Father's only Son, full of grace and truth. [15]John testified to him and cried out, saying, "This was he of whom I said, 'The one who is coming after me ranks ahead of me because he existed before me.'" [16]From his fullness we have all received, grace in place of grace, [17]because while the law was given through Moses, grace and truth came through Jesus Christ. [18]No one has ever seen God. The only Son, God, who is at the Father's side, has revealed him.

Fatima Prayer #2

My God, I believe, I adore, I hope, and I love You.

I beg pardon of You for those who do not believe, do not adore, do not hope, and do not love You.

Litany of the Blessed Virgin Mary

Lord have mercy. Christ have mercy.
>Lord have mercy.

Christ hear us.
>Christ graciously hear us.

God, the Father of heaven,
>Have Mercy on us.

God the Son, Redeemer of the world,
>Have Mercy on us.

God the Holy Spirit,
>Have Mercy on us.

Holy Trinity, one God,
>Have Mercy on us.

Holy Mary,
>Pray for us.

Holy Mother of God,[1]
Holy Virgin of virgins,
Mother of Christ,
Mother of the Church,
Mother of divine grace,
Mother most pure,
Mother most chaste,
Mother inviolate,
Mother undefiled,
Mother most amiable,
Mother admirable,
Mother of good counsel,
Mother of our Creator,
Mother of our Saviour,
Mother of mercy,
Virgin most prudent,
Virgin most venerable,
Virgin most renowned,
Virgin most powerful,
Virgin most merciful,
Virgin most faithful,

---

[1] Pray for us.

Mirror of justice,
Seat of wisdom,
Cause of our joy,
Spiritual vessel,
Vessel of honor,
Singular vessel of devotion,
Mystical rose,
Tower of David,
Tower of ivory,
House of gold,
Ark of the Covenant,
Gate of heaven,
Morning star,
Health of the sick,
Refuge of sinners,
Comfort of the afflicted,
Help of Christians,
Queen of Angels,
Queen of Patriarchs,
Queen of Prophets,
Queen of Apostles,
Queen of Martyrs,
Queen of Confessors,
Queen of Virgins,
Queen of all Saints,
Queen conceived without original sin,
Queen assumed into heaven,
Queen of the most holy Rosary,
Queen of families,
Queen of peace.
Lamb of God, who takes away the sins of the world,
    spare us, O Lord.
Lamb of God, who takes away the sins of the world,
    graciously hear us, O Lord.
Lamb of God, who takes away the sins of the world,
    have mercy on us.

Grant, we beseech Thee, O Lord God, that we, your servants, may enjoy perpetual health of mind and body; and by the intercession of the Blessed Mary, ever Virgin, may be delivered from present sorrow, and obtain eternal joy. Through Christ our Lord. Amen.

Memorare of St. Bernard

Remember, O most gracious Virgin Mary, that never was it known that anyone who fled to thy protection, implored thy help, or sought thine intercession was left unaided. Inspired by this confidence, I fly unto Thee, O Virgin of virgins, my mother; to Thee do I come, before Thee I stand, sinful and sorrowful. O Mother of the Word Incarnate, despise not my petitions, but in thy mercy hear and answer me. Amen.

Magnificat

"My soul proclaims the greatness of the Lord; my spirit rejoices in God my savior. for he has looked upon his handmaid's lowliness; behold, from now on will all ages call me blessed. The Mighty One has done great things for me, and holy is his name. His mercy is from age to age to those who fear him. He has shown might with his arm, dispersed the arrogant of mind and heart. He has thrown down the rulers from their thrones but lifted up the lowly. The hungry he has filled with good things; the rich he has sent away empty. He has helped Israel his servant, remembering his mercy, according to his promise to our fathers, to Abraham and to his descendants forever." Amen.

Angel's Prayer

"Most Holy Trinity, Father, Son, and Holy Spirit, I adore You profoundly. I offer You the most precious Body, Blood, Soul, and Divinity of Jesus Christ, present in all the tabernacles of the world, in reparation for the outrages, sacrileges and indifference by which He is offended. By the infinite merits of the Sacred Heart of Jesus and the Immaculate Heart of Mary, I beg the conversion of poor sinners."

OPENING PRAYERS

The Sign of the Cross

Before the Rosary

Come, O Holy Spirit, fill the hearts of Your faithful, and enkindle in them the fire of Your love.

V. Send forth Your Spirit, O Lord, and they shall be created.
R. And You shall renew the face of the earth.

Let us pray.

God our Father, pour out the gifts of Your Holy Spirit on the world. You sent the Spirit on Your Church to begin the teaching of the gospel: now let the, Spirit continue to work in the world through the hearts of all who believe. Through Christ our Lord. Amen.

V. You, O Lord, will open my lips.
R. And my tongue shall announce Your praise.
V. Incline unto my aid, O God.
R. O Lord, make haste to help me.
V. Glory be to the Father, etc.
R. As it was in the beginning, etc.

After the Rosary

V. Most Sacred Heart of Jesus
R. Have mercy on us.
V. Immaculate Heart of Mary
R. Pray for us.
V. St. Joseph
R. Pray for us.
V. St John the Evangelist
R. Pray for us.
V. St. Louis-Marie deMontfort
R. Pray for us.

The Catena Legionis

Antiphon.

Who is she that comes forth as the morning rising, fair as the moon, bright as the sun, terrible as an army set in battle array?

V. My soul glorifies the Lord.

R. My spirit rejoices in God, my Savior.

V. He looks on His servant in her lowliness;
    henceforth all ages will call me blessed.

R. The Almighty works marvels for me.
    Holy His name!

V. His mercy is from age to age,
    on those who fear Him.

R. He puts forth His arm in strength
    and scatters the proud-hearted.

V. He casts the mighty from their thrones
    and raises the lowly.

R. He fills the starving with good things,
    sends the rich away empty.

V. He protects Israel His servant,
    remembering His mercy,

R. The mercy promised to our fathers,
    to Abraham and his sons for ever.

V. Glory be to the Father, and to the Son and to the Holy Spirit.

R. As it was in the beginning is now, and ever shall be, world without end. Amen.

Antiphon.

Who is she that comes forth as the morning rising, fair as the moon, bright as the sun, terrible as an army set in battle array?

V. O Mary, conceived without sin.

R. Pray for us who have recourse to you. (three times)

Let us pray.

O Lord Jesus Christ, our mediator with the Father, Who has been Pleased to appoint the Most Blessed Virgin, Your mother, to be our mother also, and our mediatrix with You, mercifully grant that whoever comes to You seeking Your favours may rejoice to receive all of them through her. Amen.

CONCLUDING PRAYERS

In the name of the Father, etc.

We fly to your patronage, O holy Mother of God; despise not our prayers in our necessities, but ever deliver us from all dangers, O glorious and blessed Virgin.

V. Mary Immaculate, Mediatrix of all Graces,

R. Pray for us.

V. St. Michael and St. Gabriel,

R. Pray for us.

V. All you heavenly Powers, Mary's Legion of Angels,

R. Pray for us.

V. St. John the Baptist,

R. Pray for us.

V. Saints Peter and Paul,

R. Pray for us.

Confer, O Lord, on us, who serve beneath the standard of Mary, that fullness of faith in You and trust in her, to which it is given to conquer the world. Grant us a lively faith, animated by charity, which will lead us to perform all our actions from the motive of pure love of You, and ever to see You and serve You in our neighbor; a faith, firm and immovable as a rock, through which we shall rest tranquil and steadfast amid the crosses, toils and disappointments of life; a courageous faith which will inspire us to undertake and carry out without hesitation great things for your glory and for the salvation of souls; a faith which will be our Legion's Pillar of Fire—

to lead us forth united—to kindle everywhere the fires of divine love—to enlighten those who are in darkness and in the shadow of death—to inflame those who are lukewarm—to bring back life to those who are dead in sin; and which will guide our own feet in the way of peace; so that—the battle of life over—our Legion may reassemble, without the loss of any one, in the kingdom of Your love and glory. Amen.

May the souls of our departed legionaries and the souls of all the faithful departed, through the mercy of God, rest in peace. Amen.

For the intentions of the Holy Father.

Our Father...

Hail Mary...

Glory Be...

Act of Consecration

I, N_____, a faithless sinner, renew and ratify today in thy hands the vows of my Baptism; I renounce forever Satan, his pomps and works; and I give myself entirely to Jesus Christ, the Incarnate Wisdom, to carry my cross after Him all the days of my life, and to be more faithful to Him than I have ever been before. In the presence of all the heavenly court I choose thee this day for my Mother and Mistress. I deliver and consecrate to thee, as thy slave, my body and soul, my goods, both interior and exterior, and even the value of all my good actions, past, present and future; leaving to thee the entire and full right of disposing of me, and all that belongs to me, without exception, according to thy good pleasure, for the greater glory of God in time and in eternity.

Prayer for a personal consecration
of individuals and groups

Eternal Father, in the Holy Spirit I want to consecrate and commit myself to the Hearts of Jesus and Mary and to be a more devoted and faithful child.

Mother Mary, today I *(name)* commit myself to your Immaculate Heart. Keep me under your maternal protection and lead me to your Son Jesus.

Lord Jesus, through the Immaculate Heart of Mary, I consecrate and commit myself to Your Sacred Heart. Mould my heart after Your heart so that You will live in me ever more. Sacred Heart of Jesus and Immaculate Heart of Mary, with this consecration and commitment I return to You the love You showed me in your earthly lives, especially on Calvary, and which you show me still today. At the same time I renew my baptismal Consecration to the triune God: I renounce sin, temptation of evil and the devil; I believe in everything that God has revealed to us and which the Catholic Church teaches us.

I promise to fulfill Jesus' commandment of love for God and my neighbor, the commandments of God and of the Church and to act according to the doctrine of the Church under the successor of St. Peter. In this way I want to contribute to the unity and growth of the Church. I will personally pray the rosary with my family and other communities and observe the devotion of the first Fridays and Saturdays, making reparation for my sins and the sins of all mankind. O Sacred Heart of Jesus and Immaculate Heart of Mary, help me to accept the Gospel in my heart and to live it in faith, hope and love, that Jesus Christ will, through His cross and resurrection, become the way, the truth and the life for me. May I be nourished on heavenly bread and live out the sacrifice of the Eucharist so that I will overcome every evil and always choose life.

Full of trust, I seek shelter in your loving hearts. Protect me in all dangers and after this earthly pilgrimage take me to my eternal home in Heaven. Amen.

Twelve Sacred Heart Promises

Every First Friday of each month, devout and faithful Catholics consecrate to the Sacred Heart of Jesus in the spirit of reparation. Jesus Christ Himself made the following promises to St. Margaret Mary Alacoque, in favor of those who fervently practice and promote this devotion.

1. I will give them all the graces necessary for their state in life.

2. I will establish peace in their families and will unite families that are divided.

3. I will comfort them in all their afflictions.

4. I will be their security and refuge during life, and especially at the hour of death.

5. I will bestow abundant blessings upon all their undertakings.

6. Sinners shall find in My Heart the source, and an infinite ocean of mercy.

7. Tepid souls shall become more fervent.

8. Fervent souls shall quickly mount to great perfection.

9. I will bless every place in which an image of My Heart shall be exposed and honored and will imprint My Love on the hearts of all those who shall wear this image on their person. I will destroy in them all disordered movements.

10. I will give the priests who are animated by a tender devotion to My Divine Heart the gift of touching the most hardened hearts.

11. Those who shall promote this devotion shall have their names written in My Heart, never to be effaced.

12. I promise you in the excess mercy of My Heart that My all powerful Love will grant to all who receive Holy Communion on the First Friday of nine consecutive months, the grace of final repentance, and that they shall not die under My displeasure, nor without receiving the Sacraments. My Heart shall be their assured refuge at that last hour.

THE DOVE

I leave you with this final poem that was composed while in college many years ago as it sums up this soul's spiritual journey home.

I

Once upon a morning clear, while meditating far and near

Eagerly browsing through Your many pages of recorded word;

As I read with wisdom bringing air so filled with gentle singing,

And mystic sounds of winging, these were surely to be heard.

What is this? I inquired, brining wisdom through the written word.

What is this that I've heard?

II

It was a cold and crystal February, but ah, it was extraordinary.

And not a single thought contrary in Your written word.

Patiently I communed with heaven while the angels stirred the leaven

Invoking mercy seven sevens for the sake of all who heard.

It was our long-sought message of God's eternal Word,

Here for all to be referred.

III

And Your swift and certain Light passing through my windows' sight.

Caressing me, impressing me with wisdom rarely heard.

Your message, it was so abrupt, so that now to fill my cup.

I realized I must open up to your message that I heard.

Yes to Your anointed Holy One bringing wisdom through the word.

This thought I surely must be heard.

IV

Instantly my soul grew meeker in the presence of this speaker.
Oh great and holy messenger, with such wondrous wisdom
Thou art gird.
And so gently Thou awaken, while my ignorance is shaken
And my doubts seem so mistaken, as I ponder all I've heard.
While considering with the finite, Thy infinite illuminating word
This was surely what occurred.

V

Light so very bright in seeing, into my soul, my very being,
Exploring intellect and memories in a realm quite blurred.
As Your examining proceeded, the piercing light not once retreated.
For it was not to be defeated by accusations being slurred.
Can this really be thought I, when so gently there was was heard.
Fear not it is I God's own Eternal Word.

VI

Somehow I sensed You were no stranger approaching
at my humble manger.
Then again there came the whisper that I so long ago had heard.
Not so much as stalling, continuous the calling
Reminding of my falling and the love I had deterred
Yes gently whispering of the great fall that had occurred,
My separation from God's Eternal Word.

VII

As my heart lay open wide wondering what would come inside,

I was greeted by Your radiant and consoling One.

This pure and tranquil Dove gently filled my heart with Love

And Descending from above, encompassed that which was preferred.

Filling this cross of His until with His spirit was I gird,

Yes, forever was I gird.

VIII

Then Your purifying Dove inspired within me thoughts of love.

Yes, with Omnipotent and timeless Presence was He gird.

His beauty, dazzling white; with not a flaw to mar the sight,

Of Your conqueror of the night who would never be deterred.

For Thou spoke before all, "I Am Who Am," God's Eternal Word.

Yes forever, God's Eternal Word.

IX

I stood before Your Holy Spirit, hoping my mind might
somehow clear it.

And reveal some distant message yet unheard.

For I could not help but see, times many facets still to be,

Changing others and changing me, and all who had incurred,

The restful Presence of this solitary Bird.

The chosen messenger of God's Eternal Word

X

For Your Dove seemed quite unique, perched on us as a cross oblique

With seven last eternal cries a remembrance of His Love is heard

These last attestations traveled high through the ages by and by.

A loving and exhausted sigh was perceived while gently heard.

Tomorrow then I shall seek this Presence much preferred.

I, too, will seek God's Eternal Word

XI

All lives storms now were calm, encompassed by
Your Holy Spirit's balm.

Surely all that can be, must be in Your Word.

Passed down through the countless ages, possessing both
the seers and sages,

Explaining all the written pages of history as yet unheard.

The Almighty Father returning for His lost ones,
was not to be deterred.

Calling, calling, calling with His Eternal Word.

XII

But the accuser still was taking his allotted share of shaking

When into my troubled soul a thought occurred.

As one door closed for me to hide another opened from inside

While needed cleansing was applied, the gentle sound
again was heard.

Who is this calmly calling courier that I've heard?

Is this really God's Eternal Word?

XIII

Then Satan's call it grew much louder, inspiring thought
of being prouder,

And not humbly acknowledging Your messenger that I'd heard.

Appealing with desire for treasure and worldly comfort
without measure,

And what of my great love of pleasure: Was this not what I preferred?

So forget about this messenger calling through this gall-less bird.

And instead listen to my word.

XIV

He searched my memory like a tracker until my new found hope
grew blacker.

For his demons dug up every sin that had occurred.

They tried to fill me with despair and cause to doubt
God's love and care.

And what of that old affair and the punishment incurred?

Was I really ready to face the One I had perturbed?

Why not just listen to my word?

XV

Savior, said I, One of Love; Abba now in form of Dove.

Swiftly seeking the lost until the soul concurred.

No mountain He would not climb; my poor soul's Savior so sublime.

Traveling through the sands of time, never once is He deterred.

Calling, calling, gently calling until finally He is heard,
as God's own eternal Word.

XVI

Savior, said I, One of Love; Abba now in form of Dove.

To be sought by One as great as Thee, all seems quite absurd.

Please tell this soul what it did seek on each and every
mountain peak,

Why in distress it does wreak from the wondering it preferred?

To the One Who's heart was meek, The Son of God Who's gird.

As Your Eternal Word.

XVII

Be thy heart our sign of Love, Abba in the form of Dove.

Please forgive and take me home as if our parting had not occurred.

Cleanse my soul of every lie, dry the tear out from my eye.

Take me to Your endless sky and with Your Spirit gird.

To know, love, and serve Thee shall forever be preferred.

For thou art our Father, the great Eternal Word.

XVIII

Silently the Dove kept staring into my soul as if comparing,

My inner thoughts to my spoken words.

Then with a twinkling of an eye and a wondrous joyful cry,

I knew the meaning of that sigh that so long ago I'd heard.

I am a long-lost child of the Blessed Mother who incurred.

The everlasting Love of God's Eternal Word.

TIMELESS ROSARY REVIEWS

The very essence of prayer is lifting up our hearts and minds to God, and as we pray the Rosary and meditate on its mysteries we become ever more aware of God's love for us.

Each of the Rosaries presented here, including the Praise and Worship Rosary, Spiritual Fruit Rosary, Divine Mercy Rosary, Penitential Rosary, and Timeless Scriptural Rosary, is a beautiful prayer which blends the mysteries together and can enhance our appreciation of God's Love and the events of our Redemption. I especially like the Timeless Scriptural Rosary with its accompanying Scripture passages. It would fit in very well as a part of a Holy Hour in the presence of the Blessed Sacrament.

This booklet was obviously a great labor of Love, and I commend Brian for putting it together.

~Rev. Michael J. Burns
Pastor, Saint Mary's Church
Bordentown, NJ 08505

I always enjoyed praying the Rosary, and the Timeless Rosary helped me to open up and ponder deeply the mysteries of our redemption. It inspired me to write this little poem I've titled:

May It Be Done Unto Me
O Mary, we ponder your Rosary this day.
Open our hearts to the mysteries we pray.
And may your *fiat* well up within,
Because of Jesus your Son who died for our sin.
So dear Lady, may it be done unto me.
Because of Christ and Calvary.
May it be done unto me.
Where He has set the captives free.
May it be done unto me.

~Linda Yack, S.F.O.
Saint Mary's Church

I am so very grateful to God for the blessings and powerful presence of His Holy Spirit, which fills my heart with immense joy as I not only pray, but experience the awesome wonder of His love while contemplating all the mysteries of the *Timeless Rosary*.

I have always enjoyed praying and meditating on the mysteries of the rosary. Praying and experiencing the *Timeless Rosary* only added depth to my gratitude to our beautiful God, whose light and love illuminates the path before me in the many mysteries of His love for me.

I am left in joyful awe and wonder while being humbled by the continuous power, wisdom, and guidance of His Holy Spirit who is always there for me, just a prayer away.

Praise God!

> ~ *Deb McMullen*
> *Devoted wife, mother of five, grandmother of one,*
> *and humble daughter of our beautiful Lord*
> *November 17, 2011*

About five days a week I go to the fitness room in our clubhouse and usually spend one hour on the treadmill. Every treadmill has a television and is positioned in front of a window with a lovely view. At first I would watch TV for the one-hour workout. I soon realized that the time would be better spent praying the rosary. However, within a few months I found it difficult to maintain my focus and meditate on each mystery. Then Brian gave me a copy of his *Timeless Rosary*. Each treadmill has a ledge to place a book while working out. Although I fell in love with his "Penitential Rosary," I have prayed each of his "Timeless Rosaries." The blessings for me have been that I can now maintain my meditation while on the treadmill and I am only occasionally distracted with someone's greeting or loud laughter. I congratulate and thank Brian Horan for his wonderful book and I highly recommend you pray *The Timeless Rosary*.

> ~ *Charles F. Prettyman, Prof. Emeritus*
> *December 16, 2011*

Thank you so much for sharing *The Timeless Rosary* with us. What a blessing it is. The book makes the rosary come alive and keeps you focused on the importance and details of each decade. Please let Brian know how pleased we are with this brilliant idea for renewing our dedication to saying the Rosary (inspired by our Blessed Mother).

~Patricia Koch, Parishioner

I had to share my thoughts and emotions with you while they are fresh. I just finished *The Timeless Rosary*.

As I prayed and got into the rhythm of the prayers, I kept my journal close. When a word in the prayer stood out to me, I wrote it in my journal for further meditation. In saying *The Timeless Rosary*, the combination and blending of the illuminations (you'll get the idea when you pray it), just stirred newness within me. I found it plugging gaps while it triggered pondering, awe and wonder.

Thanks so much for introducing this new way of praying and meditating, while growing and glowing from amazement and enlightenment. Let Brian know I will keep him in my prayers and I praise God for bringing this gift of praying to us.

Thanks again, and God Bless all of you as the Spirit gently prods you into the fullness of faith and trust in Jesus. Entering into the Rosary on my own is not the same as entering in with Mary at the doorstep, ready to walk through the mysteries beside me.

~Pat Moore, Parishioner

THE TIMELESS ROSARY BEADS

● Our Father

● Ask for the gift of Faith

● Ask for the gift of Hope

● Ask for the gift of Love

Glory Be… Oh my Jesus… Announce Mysteries…
1-D, 2-D, 3-D, 4-D, 5-D *(D = Decade)*

● Our Father

● First blue bead, ask for the Holy Spirit to enlighten us in understanding the mysteries of our redemption.

The green beads represent the Joyful Mysteries

● 1-D Annunciation, 2-D Visitation, 3-D Nativity, 4-D Presentation, 5-D Finding Jesus in the temple

● On the second green bead, repeat the mystery and allow the Holy Spirit to take you deeper into that mystery.

The clear beads represent the Luminous Mysteries

○ 1-D Jesus' Baptism, 2-D Wedding Feast, 3-D Gospel, Proclamation, 4-D Transfiguration, 5-D Eucharist

○ On the second clear bead, repeat the mystery and allow the Holy Spirit to take you deeper into that mystery.

The red beads represent the Sorrowful Mysteries

- 1-D Agony in the garden, 2-D Scourging,
3-D Crowning of thorns, 4-D Carrying of cross,
5-D Crucifixion
- On the second red bead, repeat the mystery and allow the Holy Spirit to take you deeper into that mystery.

The gold beads represent the Glorious Mysteries

- 1-D Resurrection, 2-D Ascension, 3-D Descent of the Holy Spirit, 4-D Assumption, 5-D Coronation
- On the second gold bead, repeat the mystery and allow the Holy Spirit to take you deeper into that mystery.
- Last blue bead, ask for the gifts of the Holy Spirit to know God clearer, follow Him nearer, and love Him dearer.

Glory Be... Oh my Jesus...

Go back up to the next decade and announce mysteries.

Rosary Reflections

Rosary Reflections

Rosary Reflections

Rosary Reflections

ABOUT THE AUTHOR

The author's mother consecrated herself to Jesus through Mary with the Saint Louis de Montfort formula before she was married. Brian Joseph Horan would, however, take much longer to follow in her footsteps by making this same consecration himself. The fourth child of five, Horan was born in Trenton, New Jersey, in October, 1956. His father, James, and mother, Elizabeth, were both practicing Catholics and raised their children accordingly.

At age nineteen, Horan was involved in a near-fatal automobile accident, which left him with a severed ear, a broken jaw, and in a coma. His mother was called and told by the doctors to come to the hospital quickly, for they did not think he would survive. She hastily went to North Carolina with his sister, Maureen, spending the next three days praying the rosary by the author's side.

Horan came out of his coma on that third day, mumbling something about a beautiful Lady. He went on to recuperate fully and have a daughter of his own, who he named Maureen.

Brian Joseph Horan became actively involved in Catholic parish life, fulfilling roles as a Reader and an Extraordinary Minister of the Eucharist. He also became a third and fourth grade teacher at Stockton Elementary School in New Jersey.

This book is the author's small way of thanking the Blessed Mother for the love and maternal care she showed to him and to all the children her Divine Son has redeemed.

Please visit www.timelessrosary.com for more information and to purchase audio files of *The Timeless Rosary*.

About Leonine Publishers

Leonine Publishers LLC makes fine Catholic literature available to Catholics throughout the English-speaking world. Leonine Publishers offers an innovative "hybrid" approach to book publication that helps authors as well as readers. Please visit our web site at www.leoninepublishers.com to learn more about us. Browse our online bookstore to find more solid Catholic titles to uplift, challenge, and inspire.

Our patron and namesake is Pope Leo XIII, a prudent, yet uncompromising pope during the stormy years at the close of the 19th century. Please join us as we ask his intercession for our family of readers and authors.

Do you have a book inside you? Visit our web site today. Leonine Publishers accepts manuscripts from Catholic authors like you. If your book is selected for publication, you will have an active part in the production process. This book is an example of our growing selection of literature for the busy Catholic reader of the 21st century.

www.leoninepublishers.com